STRENGTH
and
GRATITUDE

STORIES OF 13 VETERAN ENTREPRENEURS

Copyright © 2021 Mark Mhley. All rights reserved. No part of this book can be reproduced in any form without the written permission of the author and its publisher.

Table of Contents

Foreword 9
Mark Mhley 17
Alyce Fernebok 51
Bobby Brown 81
Brian Rivera 95
Craig & Mark Hodder 123
Craig Washburn 137
Dan Yokoyama 151
Lionel Hines 163
Robyn Grable 183
Scott Chesson 203
Stephen White 213
Suzanne Lesko 219
Reserved for Those Who Struggle in Silence 235

Foreword

Foreword by E. Matthew Whiz" Buckley, CEO Strike Fighter Financial and TOPGUN Fighter Foundation

Everyone has a plan until they get punched in the mouth"

-Mike Tyson

I had my life figured out. Becoming an entrepreneur was not part of that plan.

In the early 1990s, I was commissioned as a Naval Officer, trained to become a Naval Aviator, and flew F/A-18 Hornets off the flight decks of aircraft carriers. I also had the privilege to graduate from the U.S Navy Strike Fighter Weapons School, popularly known as TOPGUN, and become an instructor. When I felt it was time to transition out of the Navy, like many of my brothers and sisters who earned their Wings of Gold, flying for an airline was a logical next step; it seemed the best path to my American dream of having that house in the suburbs, kids, two dogs, and the proverbial white picket fence.

One of the greatest benefits of serving your country is becoming part of a network of retired, active, and prior military service members in which one's reputation is the most valuable currency. When I left active duty service, I leveraged both that network and my reputation to land a flying job at FedEx and to continue flying the F/A-18 with the Hunters" of VFA-201, a Navy Reserve squadron located at NAS Fort Worth, Texas. My American dream would be realized through a prize job in the airline industry and flying the F/A-18 Hornet at the same time, or so I thought.

Within a few months of flying for FedEx, I realized my mind and body did not adapt well to the pace of flying all night and then trying to sleep in a hotel during the day. To remedy what I perceived to be a growing mental health and physical health concern, I sought employment with a passenger airline and was hired by American Airlines. My first flight was scheduled for September 11, 2001.

On that fateful morning, I went from preparing for my first flight with American Airlines to racing to NAS Fort Worth to try and get airborne in an armed F/A-18, ready to shoot down an airliner potentially piloted by one of my veteran brothers or sisters. Thousands of innocent American lives were taken that day, and there were countless more who had their lives turned upside down. As a result of the attacks and a weak global economy, my airline pilot career was put on an indefinite hold. For the first time in my life, I found myself without a safety net. I went from waking up on September 11th ready to work for a commercial airline to waking up on

September 12th contemplating how to avoid the unemployment line.

This period of my transition out of the Navy was extremely humbling and broadening. I became a civilian F/A-18 simulator instructor, tried my hand at acting, and when the Navy Reserve needed more from me, I took temporary orders to fly the F/A-18 with VFA-201. Fortunately, the military network showed its strength again when a colleague in the Hunters called me with an opportunity to work for an Atlanta-based military-themed consultancy, Afterburner Seminars. I jumped on this opportunity to teach business leaders that business is combat.' At Afterburner, I delivered keynote presentations and leadership seminars, based on lessons from the cockpit, to audiences ranging from the C-suite, to logistics companies, to NFL teams that went on to win the Super Bowl.

Several weeks into my job with Afterburner Seminars, I realized that a lack of leadership and teamwork skills were holding back entrepreneurs, corporate managers, and delivery teams across the country from achieving their full potential. What I took as self-evident—the leadership and teamwork skills that I and every naval aviator uses to prepare for, execute, and learn from flying every mission—our clients regarded as novel and ground breaking. Ironically, the trajectory of my own entrepreneurial future would be influenced by the lessons I learned from a client I worked with during that time, PEAK6 Investment, L.P., a volatility arbitrage equity options trading firm.

As a young officer, I invested in mutual funds and later, as an F/A-18 instructor pilot, I started to dabble in online trading and was familiar with "puts" and "calls." My basic familiarity with the market and options trading paled in comparison to the sophisticated arbitrage methods employed by PEAK6. The client, PEAK6, wasn't interested in my market and options knowledge rather, they were interested in having me "exapt" (shift the function of) the leadership and decision-making lessons from the complex environment of military aviation to the complex environment of trading and investing. I joined PEAK6 and later became the CEO of a company within that company, PEAK6 Media, LLC.

While working in Chicago with PEAK6, I learned an important lesson: the so-called "Smart" money—the investments and transactions made by expert investors—is not that smart. This lesson triggered my peanut butter cup moment as I realized two things: (1) the training methods I experienced in naval aviation could be applied to teaching investors how to trade options, and (2) the TOPGUN-grade decision-making skills I lived and coached in and out of the cockpit could help small investors outperform the Smart money.

Twelve years ago I left the familiar world of working for others and decided to become an entrepreneur. I created Strike Fighter Financial, a company that focuses on financial training and leadership consulting. Two books, a top 3% podcast in the world, an upcoming movie, a self-directed investment club, and over a thousand trained option-traders later, I am thrilled to say that my airline dreams did not come true.

The key message from my unexpected entrepreneurial story that I want to impart current and future veteran entrepreneurs with is this: becoming an entrepreneur isn t about following a plan; instead, it is about the ability to adapt to a changing and complex environment through continuous planning and learning. Like many things in life, entrepreneurship is a journey, not a destination.

I am absolutely humbled that fellow Naval Aviator and veteran-entrepreneur Mark FUN" Mhley asked me to write this foreword for Strength and Gratitude. Why? Each of the entrepreneurs you re about to read about has truly followed The Hero s Journey," and every entrepreneur or business leader can learn from their experiences. Each veteran entrepreneur began with a call to adventure when they left the ordinary civilian world to serve in the special world of the military, and experience what I call the AART of Leadership: Authority, Accountability,

Responsibility, and Trust. During their journey in uniform, they all faced situations where their AART of Leadership was tested. Today, AART is the elixir that each of these heroes brings to the entrepreneurial world.

The experiences they bring, often involving combat, are a mixed blessing. On one hand, those experiences serve to motivate them as entrepreneurs, and attract them to one another for support. On the other hand, for many who serve or served in the military, those experiences are traumatic and go unaddressed and untreated. As a result, a growing mental health crisis leaves more than 22 veterans, active-duty personnel, and reservists taking their own lives each day. In the time it takes to read this book, four to six veteran or current military members will commit suicide. This is absolutely unacceptable and is why in 2020 I started the TOPGUN Fighter Foundation, a non-profit with a mission to eliminate the stigma of mental health issues and provide our veterans access to care that works.

I m honored to introduce the stories of these 13 veteran-entrepreneurs because they demonstrate the unbeatable combination of mutual support and the AART of Leadership skills, which are not only applicable to the entrepreneur world but can also be used to address our nation s growing mental health crisis. I hope each of these stories will inspire you, help you navigate your own entrepreneurial journey, and remind you that you can t do it alone. Once we put the ladder down, and lift each other up, we re indeed stronger together.

Fight s On!

Whiz

https://www.linkedin.com/in/ematthewbuckley/
https://TOPGUNfighterfoundation.org/

CHAPTER ONE

Mark Mhley

It was a sight I was very accustomed to. But on this particular night, it was from a unique vantage, while performing a unique task. Standing on the port-side horizontal stabilizer of the Navy F-14A Tomcat, facing aft, I could make out the straight red line being drawn by the laser level along the lower portion of the port vertical stabilizer to my left. I fumbled with the white grease-pencil in my jacket pocket; in a moment, I'd use it to trace that line, and tomorrow I'd use that line to paint a one inch thick lower stripe on the stabilizer. It was a chilly but clear, January night in 2019 at the United States Naval Academy in Annapolis, Maryland. To my right, atop a stack of wooden pallets donated by Home Depot was the laser level, its tripod set to the precise height required for that lower stripe.

I was standing on an aircraft that I had become pretty close with over the past few months, as I worked to restore and repaint it to its 1988 appearance. I took in the moment, humbled by the opportunity to bring this F-14A to the Yard to create a Naval Aviation airpark and inspire generations of midshipmen to become Naval Aviators. I was also humbled by the painstaking work it was taking to repaint it; to every Navy Airframer who ever served with me in a squadron, I now have a deep appreciation for your skill and patience with paint.

It wasn't the first time I paused to appreciate the significance of the undertaking. Standing on that jet, I was literally standing on the shoulders of the giants who built the F-14 community which reared me as a young officer and Naval Flight Officer, and ingrained its warrior ethos. That ethos was grounded in teamwork, innovation, boldness, tenacity, and loyalty. Standing upon that F-14, I felt connected to that ethos again.... it was emotional....I missed being part of a high-performing team, made up of likeminded, talented individuals focused towards mission accomplishment.

Standing on that jet that night reminded me how it felt to climb out of the jet after a long flight into Iraq or Afghanistan, fist bumping my pilot before climbing down the ladder, patting the enlisted plane captain on the back, and shaking hands with the troubleshooters for their part in giving us an aircraft that safely brought us home. Standing on that jet, what I missed the most now was what I took the most for granted years before: the selfless support of my peers.

During my final year of nearly 22 years of service in the Navy, while I was an instructor at the United States Naval Academy, I led an effort to add two newly retired Navy aircraft to space currently inhabited by Vietnam era F-7J Phantom and A-4A Skyhawk jets, and to create the USNA Naval Aviation Airpark. As I retired in November 2017, we towed an EA-6B Prowler from nearby Joint Base Andrews, and the F-14A Tomcat was moved by truck to USNA in July 2018. USNA Superintendent Vice Admiral Ted Carter, whose call sign is Slapshot", allowed me to continue leading the project as a retiree, and I arranged for the F-14 to be repainted by a Navy squadron based in Virginia Beach.

That squadron worked for two cold and wet weeks in November 2018, often after dark with lights. With Thanksgiving approaching, and the jet only partially completed, they returned home. I met Slapshot at the jet the next day and told him I would finish it.

I had no business making that promise.

Thanksgiving Day 2018 began a six month effort to finish returning 162591 to her 1988 paint scheme, when Slapshot flew this actual jet as a lieutenant. This jet had a storied career; it was featured in the movie Top Gun in 1986, served in numerous squadrons, and then served out her years as an actual TOPGUN training asset before being retired in 2002, which is the year I attended TOPGUN as a student. Now, after years on display at a now-closed museum in Rhode Island, we were preparing it for its final duty as an inspiration to generations of future Naval

Aviators who will aspire to the same ethos and values which were ingrained in me.

Two months of part-time effort later, I stood on that port horizontal stabilizer on that cold January night and admired how well the laser level setup was working, but my thoughts drifted to my failing full time effort. I had retired from the Navy the year before to pursue entrepreneurship in environmental sustainability, and my entrepreneurial journey was running into challenges that I didn t know how to adapt to and overcome.

For a year, I d been working unpaid with a small group of independent contractors that were constructing an organic-waste-to-energy demonstration project for the Navy. I worked to build expertise in the field and felt that asking for pay wasn t appropriate. After I helped them secure a $640,000 grant from the state of Maryland to replicate the technology on a local beef cattle farm, I grew concerned that I was taking far more risk than any of them; they had existing businesses and devoted sporadic effort to the grant project, which I hoped to make my full-time effort. I had incorporated a business, Re4ormed Organics, as a single-person LLC to become the bio-digestion business that would ultimately include the four of us together as partners. I advocated for maintaining it as a service-disabled veteran-owned business, which would differentiate us in the market, and for keeping

51% control of the company and sharing 49% with the other three, but they pushed for equal 25% shares. I was very inexperienced in business and feared I didn t have the knowledge, skills, or tools to navigate the terrain I found myself in.

Day after day, I sought solace in my part-time spread of brushes, spray cans, stencils, and laser levels. Early in the repainting effort, solace turned to frustration, as I encountered every novice-painting challenge and failure possible.

There was something different about the frustration I felt painting that jet - it stirred up the depth of my experience in Naval Aviation, and the ethos of the F-14 community. After each painting or stencil or engineering failure, without much thought, I OODA looped it (Observe, Orient, Decide, Act); I learned, adapted, and found a solution. I built an A-frame using a small step ladder on the jet and a much taller ladder on the ground, with a reinforced wooden plank in between as my elevated platform to work off the ground. I learned stadiametric range finding to use a 1988 photograph on my smartphone to precisely position markings on the actual jet. I built a box to contain my spray paint to eliminate wind-impacts. I learned how to feather-spray-paint to avoid runs. I learned how to use transfer paper and stencils to create words and numbers. I recruited passing-by Midshipmen to help in their free time, and then a fiberglass-repair expert for a 2-hour repair. That gentleman, Scott Steele, was either inspired by the effort or had so much pity on me that he began helping with all aspects of the project until it was complete months later. He became a teammate and mentor of mine. A hockey-coaching assistant at USNA in his spare time, and a marina-manager in his full time, Scott was the Renaissance man I needed to both finish the project professionally all while relating the trials and tribulations of painting metal, coaching hockey, and mentoring midshipmen to overcoming life s bigger challenges, like pivoting a business.

Scott and I were often joined by Rear Admiral Bill Size" Sizemore to work on the jet. Size had been my Carrier Air Wing Commander during a deployment in the F-14 to Iraq in 2005, the last for the F-14 Tomcat, and was selected by Admiral Carter to have his name and call sign stenciled on the jet over one of the pilot seats, a high honor for any Naval Aviator. (Friends often asked me if my name would be stenciled on the jet, and I don t think they appreciated the significance of the act. Instead, I erected a modest memorial from my USNA Class of 1996 in the nose wheel well). Size had flight time in 162591 when it was a TOPGUN training asset before its retirement in 2002, and recalled a flight where the jet s hydraulic system failed, creating a fairly dramatic emergency, and obviously an even more dramatic story to tell years later...in front of the actual jet. It was in that moment that I realized the F-14 community's ethos focused on teamwork, innovation, boldness, tenacity, and loyalty would help me fail forward in this repainting project, just as it would in my entrepreneur-journey.

The next time Scott and I met at the jet after Size told that harrowing story, he was so excited to be working on the very jet that an admiral had a harrowing escape from death in years earlier. Scott turned to me and asked, so what's your call sign.' In the weeks I'd known him, I hadn't shared my own story of birth into the F-14 community.

I was educated by the Naval Academy, but I was raised by the F-14 community. Entering the Naval Academy in 1992, like many other 18 years olds, I aspired to become an astronaut and understood the path began with becoming a Naval Aviator. Little did I know that there are actually two categories of Naval Aviators—Navy Pilots and Naval Flight Officers—the latter role being that of a weapons, navigation, communications systems officer, and importantly, a co-pilot without stick and throttle . To qualify as a Navy Pilot, one had to have 20/20 vision, but after 2 years of being a physics major, my eyesight deteriorated to 20/200. Even with contact lenses that corrected my vision to 20/20, I was only qualified as a Naval Flight Officer (NFO), which had a track to become an astronaut just as the pilot track did. After graduating USNA in 1996, I was thrilled to be commissioned as an NFO and head to flight school in Pensacola, Florida. After two years of training, I was selected to be a Radar Intercept Officer (RIO) in the F-14 Tomcat community, and arrived at Naval Air Station Oceana in Virginia Beach to start training.

Shortly before my first F-14 flight, I was studying in the training squadron one night and took a bathroom break. Walking down the long corridor of Hangar 500, one of our instructors, Jim Bart" Bartelloni, was walking the opposite direction, stopped and asked me how I pronounced my name. It s Ma-lay, sir". Mhley," he responded, That s the most fucked up name I ve ever heard. From now on, you re FUN...Fucked Up Name."

My parents weren t amused; I think they expected the name of an animal, even if a mild tempered one. Although FUN didn t initially appeal to me either (being referred to professionally as FUN was never an aspiration of mine), it was a powerful indoctrination tool that created a new identity for me and signaled entry into this new community, which was just starting to ingrain its ethos in me.

Three years later, on the tail end of my second deployment to Iraq with Fighter Squadron TWO aboard the USS CONSTELLATION (CV-64), our nation was attacked on September 11th, 2001. I was prepping to fly in an air power demonstration over the ship for the ship s dependents cruise from

Honolulu to San Diego (the Navy calls this a Tiger Cruise"). I was shaving when I heard the news of the attacks. Much as they changed everything in and for our country, they changed the trajectory of my life.

I had applied to the Navy s Test Pilot School, which was the traditional track to become an astronaut, and felt I was a competitive candidate. In the days following the attacks, with the encouragement of my commanding officer, Kelly Booger" Baragar, our executive officer Andy Slim" Whitson, and department heads I looked up to, Jim Puck" Howe, Keith Grumpy" Kimberly, and Paul Rancho" Bernado, I decided to apply to the next TOPGUN class and become a weapons school instructor. My thinking was simple: there was a fight coming and I wanted to play a part and play it well. TOPGUN was the path to that end. Obviously, the astronaut corps has seen its share of sacrifice, but my desire to become an astronaut just felt selfish at that moment.

Many weeks later, I was notified that I was accepted into TOPGUN Class 01-02. I withdrew my application to Test Pilot School, and never looked back. The 10 week training program started in July 2002.

Between 2001 and 2005, I served first as a TOPGUN instructor at the Strike Fighter Weapons School at Naval Air Station Oceana and then as the Training Officer in one of the last F-14 squadrons, Fighter Squadron 31. The intense training of TOPGUN, followed by the responsibilities of an instructor and tactics standardization officer before, during, and after the invasion of Iraq took the warrior ethos I had been infused with and made me a standard bearer for the community. I wasn t just modeling the ethos, I was teaching the ethos, which fostered innovative, forward-leaning, adaptive, charismatic, teamwork-focused aircrew with a bias for action.

Team science defines a team as a complex adaptive system that demonstrates emergence , the concept that the whole is greater than the sum of its parts, and that interactions between team members matter more than the quality of individual members. In the 1970s and 1980s, TOPGUN leveraged this concept to develop crew coordination for F-14 aircrew to maximize their effectiveness and hence lethality of the aircraft. Designed in the 1970s, the F-14 s required a crew of two people, the pilot and the Radar Intercept Officer, to operate its complex, decoupled systems. Even after decades of system advancements, the pilot could not operate the radar and weapons system to the degree the RIO could, and the RIO could not fly the aircraft, so maximizing the capabilities of the jet in combat depended on the quality of their teamwork.

In training missions that we instructed and evaluated as TOPGUN instructors, success often came down to how well the aircrew coordinated and demonstrated emergence; did 1 + 1 equal just 2, or did they excel as a team and did a crew of 2 appear to function as a team of 4 or 5. When 1 + 1 equaled less than 2, that crew detracted from each other s situational awareness, leading to poor training performance. When 1 + 1 was equal to less than 1, accidents happened and people got hurt.

Although the stakes are not as dramatic, the concepts of teamwork and emergence apply to entrepreneurship and growing a business. Anyone who s started a business knows that one person can t do it alone, no matter the industry or type of business; we all need help in the form of mentorship, networking, and sometimes capital, and the better coordinated and consistent our team of support is, the more successful our business becomes. The question becomes, do veterans and military-spouses support each other better than our civilian friends and counterparts?

In October 2017, a month before I retired from the Navy and 15 years after serving as a TOPGUN instructor, I was selected to attending Patriot Boot Camp s 2 day entrepreneur-training program in Denver. What I saw blew me away; the F-14 community ethos was alive and well in the veteran and military-spouse entrepreneur community, which similarly fostered innovative, forward-leaning, adaptive, charismatic, teamwork-focused entrepreneurs with a bias for action. As one of the standard-bearers for this community of entrepreneurs, Patriot Boot Camp s program is grounded in the reality that each of us can't build a business alone, and as fellow-veteran entrepreneur Mario Blandini told me, we re stronger together".

What really stood out wasn t how teamwork makes the dream work". Instead, it was how quickly trust, born from shared experiences and sacrifices, grew between veteran and military-spouse entrepreneurs, which led to accelerated and more profound support to one another. Veterans and military-spouses don t just support each other better than our civilian counterparts and friends, we do it faster.

During my 2005 deployment aboard the USS THEODORE ROOSEVELT (CVN-71) with Fighter Squadron THIRTY ONE, I served as the Training Officer, responsible for training two dozen aircrew for combat operations in Iraq. During this 6-month deployment supporting coalition ground forces engaged in counter-insurgency operations as part of Operation IRAQI FREEDOM, one of these shared experiences would change my life in multiple ways.

In November 2005, we launched our first missions into Iraq. After an uneventful transit to our assigned operating area in central Iraq, I checked in with the JTAC (Joint Terminal Air Controller, who coordinated air support on behalf of the Ground Force Commander). After my standard MNPOP check in (Mission #, number of aircraft, position, ordinance onboard, playtime), the JTAC asked for our ROVER frequency. Neither my pilot nor I knew what he was referring to, so in an effort not to clobber the radio frequency with the question, I answered unable." Four hours later, back aboard the boat (what Naval Aviators affectionately call the aircraft carrier), other returning aircrew confirmed that they were asked about ROVER as well... and none knew what it was.

As a patch-wearer in the squadron (the Training Officer and any former TOPGUN trained aircrew wear a distinct TOPGUN patch on their shoulder, signifying their tactics expertise), my job was to look into things like this. Through some quick research, I found that ROVER was the Remotely Operated Video Enhanced Receiver, a laptop-and-antenna-setup that was recently embedded with American Army ground forces that provided streaming video from US Air Force F-16s supporting from overhead. Effectively, ROVER provided incredible situational awareness to our ground forces, giving then an eye-in-the-sky to peer around the next corner or building, and importantly, to help them avoid improvised-explosive-devices (which appeared on our infrared displays as hot-spots). I queried the F-14 Program Office at NAS Patuxent River over email about ROVER and within a day or two, we ascertained just how critical ROVER was to the ground forces we supported daily. Within 3 days of our first email, we developed a proposal for the Navy to approve the installation of ROVER-compatible transmitters in all 22 F-14 Tomcats on THEODORE ROOSEVELT. The beauty of it was that each jet s installation would cost only a few hundred dollars, as they would leverage off the shelf components and one trip to Radio Shack (the transmitters had been warehoused since being removed from RQ-2 Pioneer Unmanned Aerial Vehicles (UAV) which flew off US Navy Iowa-class battleships before that class ship was decommissioned in the early 1990s).

As this was planned to be the Tomcat s last deployment, we expected there would be very little support in the Naval Aviation enterprise to fund a new war fighting capability. I was about to be surprised. I pitched the proposal to my squadron Commanding Officer, Commander Rick Twig" LaBranche, and he immediately marched us down the ship s passageways to meet with the Air Wing Commander, none other than Captain Bill Size" Sizemore. Size reviewed our proposal and immediately marched our growing troupe down the passageway to meet with the Strike Group Commander, Rear Admiral Sandy Jaws" Winnefeld. Jaws reviewed the proposal and said How fast can we get this done?"

We had an installation team aboard the ROOSEVELT and all 22 F-14 Tomcats supporting ground troops with ROVER within 6-weeks of that first flight.

There is a myth that innovation and the entrepreneurial-spirit are stymied in the military and in the Navy. This entire experience, which I had the honor of sharing with then Captain Sizemore, however, busted that myth and modeled the F-14 community s ethos, which embraced innovation and aircrew with a bias towards action. These were the entrepreneurial qualities that attracted me to remain in uniform for another 12 years. 14 years after our ROVER experience, as Size accepted my invitation to come help with 162591 s repainting in 2019, I can only assume that the trust he placed in me back in 2005 remained. I m pretty sure after he said yes, he asked how fast do you want me there?"

After I transitioned from the retired F-14 Tomcat to the F/A-18F SuperHornet in 2007, I became a department head in VFA-213 and made my fifth deployment in 2009, this time to Afghanistan aboard the USS THEODORE ROOSEVELT to support Operation ENDURING FREEDOM. During each of my deployments to Iraq, with the exception of the invasion in 2003, I engaged enemy forces with weapons from our aircraft only a few times.

However, this 9 month deployment was far more kinetic. Despite increasingly stringent Rules of Engagement that limited airborne attacks to only the most dire of situations, my crew-paired pilots and I engaged insurgents on the ground a number of times in support of British troops who were taking over the security role in the Helmand Province from American Marines.

One memorable mission stands as testimony to the value of trust, not for what we did as a crew, but for what we didn t do.

A few months into the deployment, I was flying a support mission for a routine British ground patrol with Lieutenant Jason Tike" Gustin, whom I d trained alongside and flown with dozens of times in the previous year. Our crew coordination and our trust in each other was strong. And that day, that trust would be tested, and a decision we made remains the best one of my life.

After an uneventful hour orbiting over their position, the patrol came under fire from a nearby structure; not an uncommon event. We had been in communications with the patrol and together were able to fix their attacker s location, which the British patrol quickly subdued on their own.

As I began to scan the surrounding area with our infrared targeting pod, I located a group of adults about 2 kilometers away moving rapidly towards the British patrol. On my 10 inch by 10 inch display, the black and white image didn t give away if these were insurgent reinforcements moving to help their stricken-comrades, or were these curious, innocent locals coming to see what just happened. I reported what we were tracking, and Tike and I were surprised to get an immediate clearance to attack the group from the British. As we reacted as trained, and prepared our aircraft to release a laser guided bomb on the group, I noticed how disciplined this group was...they were following each other, using cover and concealment as they snaked through the terrain and around buildings. I also noticed they seem to be carrying equipment in backpacks. Our British patrol again confirmed there were no other friendly patrols in the area.

Tike and I discussed what we saw with each other—weak signals that something wasn t right—but we still looked for opportunities to make our attack. Our British patrol asked the status of our attack and I responded standby". Tike and I assessed we had about 5 minutes to respond before this group would become a small-arms threat to the British patrol. Each minute, the British patrol asked again, each time more urgently. Each time, I replied with a more confident standby." The weak signals weren t strong enough for us to call off our attack, but were strong enough to cause us to delay it as long as possible. Restraint in using force was a key part of the rules of engagement, and we simply trusted each other in our cockpit more than the British patrol and their perception of a threat.

All of a sudden, a new British voice came up on the radio...one we hadn t heard yet. It was another British patrol returning to base, whose position correlated with the group we d been tracking. We had almost killed all of them.

I took a deep breath, asked if we could be of any further service, and within moments we checked off the frequency, and returned to the ship.

Had Tike and I not trusted each other that day, had we not shown restraint and instead done as we were directed, we would have taken the lives of 12 young British soldiers—who probably never knew how close they came to death.

Today, as an entrepreneur, I understand that the trust that service-members grew with each other during shared-experiences and struggles (if not sacrifices), like occurred for me in 2009, accelerates trust between veteran and military-spouse entrepreneurs today, whether we served together or not, and this accelerates and deepens our support to one another.

At the completion of my time as a department head, my performance evaluations were not going to lead to aviation command. Through a chance encounter with a fellow aviator at my gym one afternoon, I learned about an opportunity with a SEAL team in Virginia Beach, applied, and was surprised to be hired into their operations department along with one of my good friends from my days at Fighter Squadron TWO, CDR Richard Tex" Kelly.

For 4 years I worked alongside the finest warriors and leaders in our entire military, on some of the most sensitive and high-risk operations. This period of my career reinforced my understanding of trust, relationships, innovation, a bias for action, and more. There is much common ground between the Naval Special Warfare community ethos and the Navy Strike-Fighter and F-14 ethos I reflected on earlier, as both are high-performing teams that take full advantage of concepts like emergence. For the sake of classification and brevity, but hardly to overlook this incredibly rewarding and impactful period of my life, let s move into 2013, when I was fortunate to be assigned to the United States Naval Academy s Political Science Department, where I would teach for the next 4 years. While there, I became the Deputy Director of Humanities and Social Sciences, helped to run the naval aviation training, recruiting, and education program, all while teaching political science. I also hatched a crazy idea to move an EA-6B Prowler and F-14 Tomcat onto the Yard to build an airpark.

I retired from the Navy in November of 2017 after 21.5 years of service. Two months prior, during my terminal leave, I was on camping trip in the Challis National Forest in Idaho and made the decision to start a business in Annapolis, focus on sustainability, and build jobs for veterans. Weeks after I retired, we towed the EA-6B from Joint Base Andrews to the

Yard, craned it into place, and had a Marine Corps Prowler squadron repaint it. With the Tomcat move planned for July 2018, I committed myself to finish building the USNA Naval Aviation Airpark while embarking on my entrepreneurial journey.

Fourteen months later, on that cold night in January 2019, I stood on the port horizontal stabilizer of 162591. I reflected on three exceptional events and extraordinary opportunities that helped my transition into entrepreneurship and my business pivot, and deepened my connection with the veteran community. Little did I know I was standing on the fourth.

The first was Patriot Boot Camp s (PBC) program in Denver in September 2017. This entrepreneur training event showed me that including military-spouses with veterans was a powerful way to strengthen the entire military family. The two mutually-supportive groups demonstrate accelerated-trust", born from their shared experiences and sacrifices, and PBC leverages this during a rapid-fire, two-day program to enable mutual-support long lasting after the event.

The inclusion of military-spouse entrepreneurs is hardly cosmetic. On the second day of the program, military-spouse Laura Early and her company, Wise Advisors, won the PBC pitch contest. It was obvious that everything I did in the future that supported veterans had to also support military spouses.

A year and a half later, another key event that connected me back to the veteran community was also an unexpected lesson in failing forward. This one was taught by a billionaire that led me to a pause and a pivot.

In 2018, I joined a small team involved in the research and development of organic-waste-to-energy technology for the Navy. I didn t feel I had the skills that would merit pay, and I didn t want to financially burden them, so I served as an unpaid intern, learning construction, mechanical engineering, chemistry, and energy production. I had recently sold my house in Virginia Beach, and along with my retiree-pension, felt I could sustain my existing quality of life. In the short term, I felt it was a tenable relationship and situation.

In May 2018, I developed and wrote a grant that won a $640,000 grant from the Maryland Energy Administration to replicate the Navy technology on a beef-cattle farm in Harford County, Maryland. The grant was awarded to the sole-proprietor that held the Navy s contract (and hence had the experience-in-industry that I did not) and other unassociated business, and so in May 2018 our plan was for me to found a business, Re4ormed Organics, to manage and operate this first farm digester, and to develop and seek funding for future projects. I was the sole-member of the LLC, and planned to bring in the other three team members as partners before the project construction was complete.

The summer of 2018 was an exciting time, and I was proud to share Re4ormed Organics mission, which was to address food waste that otherwise ends up in landfills and farm-animal waste that causes destructive runoff throughout the Chesapeake Bay watershed. I came across the StreetShares Veteran Small Business Award focused on the food and beverage industry, sponsored by the Boston Beer Company, and it seemed like an ideal way to get the word out about Re4ormed Organics and maybe even win some of the $25,000 of prize money. I really wasn t all that interested in connecting with the veteran-entrepreneur community, but more so the broader sustainability-minded business community—and the idea of winning some prize money sounded good too.

I made a short pitch video and was humbled to become one of the 3 finalists through an online voting campaign. At the September 2018 Military Influencer Conference (MIC) in Orlando, I was voted by fellow veteran and military-spouse entrepreneurs as the first place winner of the live-pitch contest. The entire MIC event showed me how genuinely powerful the veteran and military-spouse entrepreneurs community was in support of each other s business-growth. As it turned out, my PBC experience wasn t an anomaly.

As part of the StreetShares first prize, I traveled to Boston in February 2019 to have a mentorship-meeting with Jim Koch, founder of the Boston Beer Company, and his entire executive team. To prepare for the meeting, I read Jim s book, Quench Your Own Thirst, updated our grant-funded project pro forma, and met with another mentor of mine, John Sohl, who gave me tips on how to make best use of 2 hours with a billionaire.

Jim Koch is one of the smartest, most genuine, and attentive leaders I ve ever spent time with. After carefully reviewing every aspect of my situation, and relating it to his own, he saw excessive risk in our grant-funded effort, and his advice was profound: pause my involvement in the project development, evaluate how much runway I had left (financially and motivationally), and don t be afraid to fail-forward and pivot away from this effort to something else. He urged me to protect Re4ormed s ability to become certified as a service-disabled veteran owned business in the future, and to not dilute ownership of the company now.

In 2 hours, Jim validated all of my concerns. Soon after I returned to Maryland, I relayed my concerns and gracefully parted with my colleagues. I had no idea how I d pivot my business or what the word

Organics" might be replaced by in my business name, but I hoped it would become something that supported the community that had supported me.

The next morning, I woke up and drove out to the F-14 at USNA to put in a full day s work on the jet. That week, my focus was on fixing the ejection warning triangles under the canopy that were originally painted in the wrong places. I built a box that attached to the jet to me help spray paint stencils without worrying about winds. I was adapting, overcoming, and demonstrating the ideals the community that raised me.

For weeks, I focused on finishing this repainting project. I connected with Scott Steele, who professionalized our effort, and Admiral Sizemore, who joined us weekly and exuded the ideals of the F-14 warrior ethos when I most needed it...as I was pivoting my business.

The third event and opportunity came in April 2019, when I was selected into the 2019-2020 Global Good Fund (GGF) Veteran Leadership Program, focused on supporting veteran social entrepreneurs through leadership and executive coaching. My first leadership coaching session couldn t have come at a more critical time. When I met Gary Slyman first over the phone, I was struck again by the selflessness the veteran community shows its own in need. A USNA graduate and former Marine Corps Aviator,

Gary worked in education administration and then began his own leadership coaching practice, and was now aligned with the Commit Foundation and the Global Good Fund to deliver transitioning veterans his coaching. I shared the ups and downs of my entrepreneur journey of the previous year and a half, that I needed help pivoting the business, and probably shared more than he wanted to hear about the restoration and repainting of a Navy F-14 Tomcat at USNA.

At the May 2019 GGF Gala event breakfast, I fortuitously sat next to Larry Glick, one of GGFs executive mentors and a partner in a merchant credit card business. We exchanged our backgrounds and I shared my current challenges and pivot into the unknown. Larry handed me his business card and said If you d like to talk about partnering to deliver our credit card services to your veteran community, give me a call." A month later, I took him up on his offer.

That night I met Larry, two weeks before we finished repainting the F-14, my 6 year old dog, Donner, was hit and killed by a pickup truck in my neighborhood. As my closest friends know, Donner had been my most loyal companion before and during all of the uncertainly of my transition out of the Navy and into entrepreneurship. In a moment, my entire world fell apart.

Three days later, my second meeting with Gary unpacked everything that had happened. I mourned the loss of a dog that pushed me on running trails as in life. I realized how important staying connected with the veteran and military-spouse entrepreneur community was for me, and how much impact I could make on that community if I shifted towards a strategic focus. Together, we set three goals that would define Re4ormed s new mission:

1. Connect veteran and military-spouse business owners to the resources they need to launch and grow their businesses,

2. Shift my approach to leadership from the operational to the strategic realm, and

3. Develop veterans, military spouses, and their businesses.

With the F-14 project, I had failed-forward by adapting and overcoming every challenge thrown my way; now I needed to fail-forward in entrepreneurship by adapting, innovating, and aggressively finding ways to pay forward everything I had learned through failure during the previous year and a half.

Failing forward as an entrepreneur and pivoting Re4ormed mirrored my experience with the F-14 project. Success in both took accepting that failure is inevitable and it should be celebrated as an opportunity to learn and do it better (hence the name failing-forward), and that real-impact is indeed the sum of a million imperfections.

We grappled with every possible paint malfunction on the F-14. Celebrating those failures was akin to torture, and we often didn t get it exactly right. But as Scott Steele reminded me, perfection is the enemy of completion; it s not attainable in paint (or in much of anything worthwhile). Each time we finished painting a part of the jet, Scott had me step back to where the average visitor would stand, where the whole was greater than the sum of its imperfect parts; it was truly beautiful and perfect-enough .

Rebuilding Re4ormed required the same approach: focus on building impact among veteran and military-spouse entrepreneurs, leverage and respect their innate, accelerated trust with one another, and everything else (including revenue) will follow. Certainly, details such as the website, the branding, and customer engagement emails were important towards creating impact, but first I had to grow a space where these entrepreneurs could leverage that trust to support each other and grow business partnerships and deals faster.

I also had to call Larry Glick of Integrity Merchant Solutions, and within minutes we had built the framework for Re4ormed s first partnership delivering back-office services to veteran and military-spouse entrepreneurs.

Into the winter of 2020, I focused my effort on growing my network of veteran and military-spouse entrepreneurs, both in my hometown of Annapolis, Maryland and nationally, and my reputation among them as a trusted source of support. My GGF executive coach, retired Marine General Drew Davis taught me to take advantage of every lead and every contact that s offered to you, and put your best effort into each, as you never know where they ll lead. So, I got involved in everything that had the word veteran in it. I attended the inauguration of Maryland s Veteran Chamber of Commerce, I became a member of my county veterans commission (an advisory role to the county executive on issues germane to the veteran population), and I created a veteran and military-spouse small business spotlight series on social media that brought attention to an entrepreneur every week. I also joined two local veteran entrepreneurs, Adam Bixler and Jeff Mund, and a military-spouse entrepreneur who was the executive director of Patriot Boot Camp, Jen Pilcher, to discuss how to better support and grow our local community of entrepreneurs, which seemed small in number and uncoordinated. It frustrated me that finding a networking happy hour for veteran entrepreneurs required a drive into Washington, DC or Northern Virginia. So, I organized a veteran and military-spouse entrepreneur ecosystem initiative in coordination with state and local government representatives, as well as local entrepreneurs. Our kickoff meeting in early February successfully began to organize our regional ecosystem of veteran and military-spouse entrepreneurs and the resources available to help them launch and grow their businesses, and we scheduled our first networking happy hour event for mid-April.

In March 2020, the Covid-19 pandemic swept across the nation and we adapted by adjusting the networking event to be a virtual event via Zoom. We shared the invitation to this Annapolis All Call" for veterans and military-spouses in the Annapolis area and beyond to come pitch their businesses. We were so surprised to have 105 people from all over the country register, and it went so well, that we held them every two weeks before shifting to a monthly schedule.

A few weeks after that first All Call , attendees began to approach me to partner with Re4ormed to help deliver their services to this community of entrepreneurs. This confirmed my efforts to build trust across the community was succeeding, and I hustled to create a website for Re4ormed; after months of being strategically focused, it was time to operationalize the business.

In September, the monthly All Call Series was expanded to Texas with the help of veteran-entrepreneur Mario Blandini, Minnesota, and we added a quarterly National Non-Profit All Call. That same month, with five business partnerships in place, I set a goal to grow them to 50 within a year. By January 2021, Re4ormed had 20 partnerships in its family of back-office service-providers, and by September 2021 that number grew to 32 services and 20 product vendors,.

Every aspect of the business began to grow at the same time. The All Call Series added monthly events in Colorado and the Pacific Northwest, and after I attended Dartmouth's Tuck School of Business' 'Next Step' program in April 2021, we added elite-athletes to our community of support. 'Next Step ' brought together transitioning veterans and elite-athletes (those who competed for Team USA in their sport), and the shared ethos and values made it apparent that we veterans have much to share with this under-supported community that wore our nation's cloth in competition.

To help manage all of these events and relationships, I turned to our virtual-assistant partner, Freedom Makers, and hired my first part-time assistant, Army-veteran and spouse Sydney Hoben, in June 2021. Along with a deep understanding of the veteran and military-spouse community, Sydney brought a level of creativity and organization to

Re4ormed that I only dreamed of a year prior. Her inclusion on our team was transformational.

Re4ormed s growth and success are owed to how we accelerate trust born from shared experiences, struggles, and sacrifices. Trust is grown from the exchange of increasingly larger amounts of risk between individuals, and our shared qualities allow veterans and military-spouses to achieve trust in a fraction of the time it takes our civilian counterparts.

Our family of business services has been successful because clients trust the work Re4ormed does to vet and then integrate each of these veteran and military-spouse services, which saves the client time needed to search, interview, and compare services. When a client adopts one of our partner services, they not only get an affordable, high-quality service, they also get mentored by a fellow veteran or military-spouse business owner who wants to help them thrive.

The All Call Series has been successful because of the accelerated mutual-support, partnerships, and the business deals that occur through these no-cost forums. All of that is owed to how we build and leverage trust: the accelerated-trust among attendees, and trust in Re4ormed to deliver an impactful forum that helps them thrive.

Thank you to all of the veteran and military-spouse entrepreneurs who have joined the Re4ormed ecosystem to support one another, especially the other veterans whose stories are told in this anthology. Your selflessness and your ability to accelerate-trust with one another are remarkable. The ecosystem we have formed truly demonstrates the power of emergence, that there is beauty in the sum of our individual efforts, that we are indeed stronger together.

Today, when I pass the F-14 at the Naval Academy, I m reminded of how critical a role in my transition and in my business-pivot that project played. I owe thanks to Scott Steele for his patience and tutoring, Size Sizemore for reconnecting me to the F-14 warrior ethos, Gary Slyman for helping me visualize the pivot and create Re4ormed s new goals, and my dog, Donner, for never letting me slow down on the tough climbs on his favorite trail.

I hope you're inspired by the stories of the veteran entrepreneurs that follow, and that each one gives you the strength to get up your toughest climbs.

Mark Mhley is a retired Naval Officer who spent nearly 22 years in uniform. After graduating from the U.S. Naval Academy in 1996 Mark was designated a Naval Flight Officer and graduated from the Navy Fighter Weapons School, TOPGUN, in 2002. Mark completed five deployments as an aviator in the F-14 Tomcat and F/A-18 Super Hornet while supporting operations around the globe including SOUTHERN WATCH, IRAQI FREEDOM, and ENDURING FREEDOM. After serving at the Naval Special Warfare Development Group (NSWDG) in Dam Neck, Virginia from 2010-2013 he had the pleasure of returning to the U.S. Naval Academy as the Deputy Director of the Humanities and Social Sciences Division and Senior Naval Flight Officer before retiring in 2017. After retiring, Mark founded Re4ormed Organics, a food and farm-animal waste recycling company that commercialized anaerobic digestion technology pioneered by the Navy. In 2018, The StreetShares Foundation and Boston Beer Company awarded Re4ormed the 2018 Veteran Small Business Award in the food and beverage industry and in 2019 Mark was recognized as a Global Good Fund Veteran Leadership Fellow. Mark pivoted Re4ormed in 2019 to help veteran and military spouse entrepreneurs launch and grow their businesses and nonprofits. In 2021, Mark attended Tuck Business School s Next Step Program for transitioning service-members and elite-athletes, which led Re4ormed to include elite-athletes in their community of support.

Mark Mhley
Commander, USN, Retired
www.Re4ormed.com
https://www.linkedin.com/in/mark-mhley/
Info@Re4ormed.com

CHAPTER TWO

Alyce Fernebok

My family, school, friends, life experiences and time in service as a Marine and a veteran are all contributors to what I stand for – my purpose, my values, my spirit and my identity. And, I believe that my company embodies my whole person. To have a successful company, it must reflect who I am.

It all started with Wonder Woman. I was born in 1974, and I watched Wonder Woman with my dad from the ages of two to five years old. I wore Wonder Woman Underoos, reflected bullets with my bracelets, compelled people to tell the truth, gave my friends all my toys (that is how a five-year old sticks up for the little guy), spun in circles and loudly, repeatedly and incorrectly sang Wanda Wah-mon" from the show s theme song refrain at the top of my lungs while I ran in my Underoos through my house and yard. If these references don t jog any memories, watch some of the old shows. In the original Wonder Woman, Diana s disguise is as a Navy Yeoman Petty Officer First Class. Wonder Woman is also the pilot of an invisible plane. Thanks to Wonder Woman and my dad, the seed was planted. I am a tall woman. While I currently stand at 5 11", in college and through most of my 20 s, I was six foot tall. So it should be easy to imagine that I was a giant kid and the biggest kid in my class until the eighth grade. I was the anti-bully." The guiding principles that my father instilled in me, combined with the imagery of Wonder Woman established a very clear guideline for me regarding the kind of person I should be. This included sticking up for the kids who couldn t stick up for themselves.

In high school, my basketball coach reinforced those principles and ideals, and as far as teenagers go, I think my parents got pretty lucky. My basketball coach also created the opportunity for me to go to the Naval Academy. I had to finance college using my own resources, and I was looking for basketball scholarships. I was going to basketball camps in the summer and getting some looks and letters from colleges. Then my basketball coach, Coach Crutchfield, grabbed me one day my junior year and said, Alyce you have to go to the Naval Academy. Yes you got to go to the Naval Academy." He had a smile on his face and a look that made it clear that he was pleased with his revelation. When Crutch was excited about something, the cadence of his words would increase, and the pitch of his voice would get high. My standard response to anything Crutch said to me was smile and shrug and OK."

I had never heard of the Naval Academy, but if Crutch thought it was something for me, then I was open to it. I had a strong and loving friendship with Crutch, and I felt close and trusted him like he was my father. He followed up my acknowledgement with, I m going to call Coach Smalley". He was the current athletic director and former women s basketball coach at the Naval Academy at the time. Next thing I knew, basketball coaches were visiting me and my parents at my home, and I had a United States Naval Academy information book and an overnight visit scheduled. I walked through the visitor gate of the Naval Academy by Halsey Field House, where the women s team practiced, and the moment I stepped onto the campus, I felt I belonged there. I knew in my heart that I would go to school at the Naval Academy and that it was my destiny. I didn t apply to any other colleges. When I think back, I can t believe that my parents let me get away with a love at first sight, this is my destiny approach," to applying to college, but I am so grateful now that they did because this gave me permission to always trust my heart. I had no idea what I was getting into but the mission of the Naval Academy resonated with my inner Wonder Woman: "To develop Midshipmen morally, mentally and physically and to imbue them with the highest ideals of duty, honor and loyalty in order to graduate leaders who are dedicated to a career of Naval service and have potential for future development in mind and character to assume the highest responsibilities of command, citizenship and government."

So, there I was on July 01, 1992, I-day (I is for Indoctrination.), at the Naval Academy – fresh, goofy haircut, clueless, confused and sworn into the Navy. That day when we all stood together and raised our hands to serve was the first day of the strongest, most loving relationship in my life. This does not take away from my family or the other beautiful friendships I have developed over my life and my strong bonds with the Marines and sailors. I have served with, but there is something different about the closeness I have with my friends from school.

I DID NOT excel as a midshipman. In fact, I was a disaster plebe. Plebe is what a freshman at the Naval Academy is called. Our freshman summer and year is a physical and mental harassment package similar to boot camp. As a plebe, you are supposed to remember daily rates that include weather, the menu for the meals in the chow hall, events, athletic scores, etc. We also had military information that we were supposed to be able to report whenever asked, such as the name and designation of all the CVN class carriers in the fleet and their commissioning date. We had personal uniform and room inspections daily and were constantly asked rates" memorized from a small book called Reef Points that contained poems and Navy lore. Whenever we were asked a question by an upperclassman, we were expected to shout out the answer without hesitation. For example, as a plebe, an upper class could ask me, Midshipman Fernebok, How s the cow?" I was supposed respond loudly and succinctly with the answer Sir, she walks, she talks, she's full of chalk. The lacteal fluid extracted from the female of the bovine species is highly prolific to the....." I personally never remembered any more than the she walks she talks portion and then would just start doing push-ups. To relay this story, I had to Google the answer to the cow question so I could write it in this chapter.

I was a mess. I was struggling hard in my academics, and I didn t have the time to study my daily rates. I was physically exhausted from practicing and playing basketball and mentally exhausted from the stress of academic failure. Adding to this was an intense basketball travel schedule in my freshman year, and I was missing a lot of school. My poorly advised approach was to stay up late to study, but that would cause me to fall asleep in class and get more behind. My roommate, Ann, tried to help me and stayed up drilling me with my rates and tutoring me on my studies, but my tired brain couldn t absorb the information. I got an academic board after my first semester because I had a grade point average of

0.17. In an academic board, you are evaluated to determine if you are going to be kicked out of school for substandard academic performance. I think I was failing all my subjects except physical education. As it turned out, I was on academic probation and summer school my entire four years of school.

After my freshman year, academics continued to be a challenge for me, but things got better. Luckily for me, everything at school wasn t about academics or my freshman year. We were also evaluated on how we performed in the execution of military type tasks and leadership. There are programs during the summer that allow you to experience different occupations in the military and be evaluated to determine your aptitude to perform in different military specialties. Besides the academics and physically demanding schedule, I also experienced harsh judgment, and dislike toward me for the first time because I was female. This was very confusing to me as an 18 year old. I wasn t raised with gender bias or gender roles. I didn t even know such a thing existed, but I had to begin figuring out how to deal with it because as I know now, it wasn t going to ever go away.

After getting through my freshman year, I could start thinking about the career I wanted in the fleet. I knew I wanted to have a combat mission. That s what was strong in my heart. However, for the first two years of school, combat specialties were not open to women. On April 28, 1993, then-Secretary of Defense Les Aspin released a memorandum directing the military departments to open more positions to women and establishing an implementation committee to review and make recommendations on such implementation issues. Several months later, as part of the National Defense Authorization Act for FY 1994 (P.L. 103- 160), Congress enacted language that repealed the remaining prohibitions on women serving on combatant vessels and aircraft. This meant Marine Corps Aviation would be open to women.

If I could secure a Marine Corps aviation slot, then I would be guaranteed a combat mission. Luckily for me, the Naval Academy had recently introduced a review process for service selection that wasn t based solely on class rank. This meant that academic boneheads like me could compete based on an interview process and other criteria, such as our performance during summer training events. For those of us interested in the Marine Corps, we did a summer event called Leatherneck. It was fun, running around the woods with camouflage on, doing land navigation, shooting guns, working through military problems and operations with my friends. This was my JAM! I did receive a Marine Corps Aviation billet when I graduated from the Naval Academy as a 2ndLT in May, 1996 and then shortly headed to The Basic School that summer.

The Basic School is the first professional training that all Marine Corps officers receive before they begin training in their specialty. I am incredibly proud to tell people I m a Marine. I believe in the Marine Corps values of Honor, Courage and Commitment, and I strive to embody those values in my actions. Marine is part of my identity. I am not always a perfect Marine, but I always try to live up to those values and standards. During my active duty service, I had a really fun, exciting and challenging occupation specialty: CH-46 E helicopter pilot. I did not step into a career field that had just opened to women blindly. I knew it would be a challenge. In fact, during one of my summer cruises, I spent some time at a Huey squadron, and one time when I walked into the ready room, a small group of pilots I encountered told me that they didn t want me there, and the squadron was no place for a woman.

It was such a hostile environment that after that trip, I changed my service selection wish list when I got back to school and removed the Marine Corps. When I did this, the Senior Marine at the Naval Academy asked to speak with me. I told him what had happened, and he told me that I would experience the same thing in the Navy and that this was something I would have to face down no matter where I went. He convinced me to keep my focus on the Marine Corps. As I mentioned earlier, I had already had a small introduction to this general dislike of females at the Naval Academy. The difference was that at school I was protected by my friends and classmates. I had a support structure, and we were all connected. So even if there were some jerks and a culture of machismo, I had my friends to protect and support me. After graduation, we all started to separate, and our tight group diluted because we mixed into the rest of fleet and the corps. Through The Basic School and flight school, things felt good. I was still surrounded by friends, sand we were all in training working towards the same goal graduating from flight school, receiving our designation as a Naval Aviator (getting our wings) and FINALLY getting to our first Marine Corps or Navy squadron.

When I got to my first squadron, I had landed in a great one. My helicopter wasnt invisible, like Wonder Woman s plane, but it was still really cool. Some of our squadron helicopters were so old they were flown in the Vietnam War. I loved it. The senior pilots there were professional; they taught me and only cared that I became an excellent pilot. They fully welcomed me into the fold, and my CO and XO were great examples of leadership. They evaluated their Marines based on competency and performance, not gender. But then we got a new CO and XO. We began our work up, and other pilots joined our squadron to form the aviation component for deployment. After we deployed, things changed. I don t know what it was that caused the change. I believe it was boredom and isolation combined with poor leadership.

On deployment, I was the subject of several very explicit sexual rumors. Rumors that were given legitimacy and not stopped by the leadership in my squadron or on the ship. When I would walk into the officer s mess, I could hear and see the chittering among my fellow pilots. It was embarrassing, so I stopped going to chow or would try to go at times that would be off hours so I wouldn t have to see people. After I returned from deployment, this type of talk and rumors about me and my sex life increased. On one occasion upon picking up my roommate from the officer s club after he had been drinking, fellow and senior officers cat-called me and made sexual innuendos about me and my roommate. I heard people make comments about me on the other line of work calls. I got in fights on the phone, screaming and demanding the identity of the voices I heard in the background. I was threatening to fight them.

In private, I started crying a lot., mostly when I was alone in my car. I cried on my way into work, and I cried on my way home. I hated every day. Today I think about how I was feeling during that point in my life. That was a very difficult time for me, as a young woman, early to mid-twenties, and I felt very alone, I didn t have my close friends with me, and no one stuck up for me. Nor I did know how to navigate that experience emotionally because the experience wasn t in keeping with who I was or what I stood for. I did not retain any close relationships from the years I was in the Squadron. I was humiliated, and all I could think about was how to get out.

One senior officer knew I was struggling and suggested that I look for a duty assignment as the senior Marine officer at the Navy SERE School. SERE stands for Survival Evasion Resistance and Escape. SERE was my escape from Marine Aviation, and I set my heart on it. The Marine that was currently assigned at SERE was coming to the end of her term, and it was slated for a Marine Aviator with no restriction on the job for women. When I first applied for the job, the Marine Corps detailer told me I couldn t have the job because a female woman aviator currently had the job, and if I got it subsequently, it would turn it into woman s work,"

61

a woman s job. Know that my father and I are close. He always has been my hero dad, and I have always been his hero girl. When I relayed my disappointment to him that I wouldn t get the job and I told him why, my dad got PISSED! When my dad gets mad, it gets serious and a little frightening. He told me he was going to initiate a congressional inquiry. When my father told me he was writing Representative Morella, who had given me my appointment to the Naval Academy, I told him not to. I was scared. I told him there would be backlash. I told him everyone would hate me. I told him it would ruin my career. He did it anyway. He did not allow me to let fear close me down. I think he saw my heart was broken and that I had lost my strength and my ability to fight for myself.

He courageously fought for me, removed obstacles to my happiness and led me with his love. He took a stand, and he wrote Representative Morella, and the inquiry got initiated. I ended up getting the job and going to work at SERE school, which was the shining star of my time in service. Everything I expected, learned and hoped for as a leader in the Marine Corps came true during my time at the Navy SERE School. When I arrived in 2002, it was also the first time since 1999 that I was stationed with another officer that I knew from the Naval Academy, Suzanne Lesko, another veteran contributing to this book. After my experience in the squadron, having someone that I was already connected with and that I could trust was hugely supportive and helpful to me. At SERE, I was in charge of a small detachment of Marines and became the training officer and eventually the operations officer. I worked closely with my Leading Chief Petty Officer (LCPO) and my Staff Non-Commission Officer (SNCO). We would grab lunch and talk about work. We had regular meetings and worked together to lead and professionally develop our Sailors and Marines. We would even go for a run or bike ride on occasion – normal stuff I had regularly seen other male officers do with their LCPO or SNCO.

This experience for me was HUGE because I did those things and never got accused of a sexual impropriety like I had when I was in the squadron. I simply worked hard and did a good job. I took care of my Sailors and Marines, and for three years at the Navy SERE school, I had the experience I was hoping for in the military and as a Marine. I loved working there. I excelled. It was the best job I will ever have in my life. If I could have stayed there forever with those Sailors and Marines, I would have. My LCPO, Chief Kuttler, a Navy SEAL, asked me to be his retiring officer. This was the greatest honor of my military career. We are still in touch and close today.

When my SERE School tour was coming to an end, it coincided with my nine years of obligation to the Marine Corps. After my great experience at the SERE school, taking care of my Sailors and Marines and being appreciated for the quality of my work and performance as an officer, I did not want to go back to Marine Aviation. So I got out of the Marine Corps. Because of my performance and SERE school, I was offered a job to work as a contracted civilian in the Army s Special Operations Division on the Army Staff located in the Pentagon. My specific task was to build a robust Personal Recovery Program to include SERE in the regular Army, civilian and contractor training programs. Prior to that, Personal Recovery and SERE training was only offered to Special Forces in the Army. Three years of a positive supportive experience at SERE school was all it took to rebuild my confidence and give me some perspective about my experience dealing with men in my squadron. I rolled into my new job on the Army Staff feeling fearless. I was the only woman working in the G-3 Operations Division except for the Colonel s civilian executive assistant. This is the time I started to thrive. I was respected. I had no limits. I regularly developed and briefed implementation plans to my division s leadership, a one-star General, the Army G-3, a two-star General, and the Vice Chief of Staff of the Army a three-star General. I was 30 years old.

The Soldiers I worked with in the Special Operations Division supported me, and the two Colonels I worked for during my term there mentored and looked out for me. I m still in touch with many of them, and I have often told them that they are a few of the best Marines I have ever worked with. That is the best compliment I could give a Soldier. The next seven years of my civilian life were golden. I learned my new trade. I figured out how the Army, the Joint Staff and the Offices of the Secretary of Defense work and learned the ins and outs of contracting with the federal government. In addition, I received several leadership opportunities working for three different companies to learn about how government contracting companies work, and I got to experience a variety of company sizes and cultures. I was always looking for opportunities to do new work and learn new things and worked extremely hard and very long hours. That meant often arriving at work before the sun was up and leaving after it was dark year round. The work I was doing for the Army felt meaningful, and I was very successful.

In 2013, I was emotionally burnt! I was recovering from a very nasty, stressful and expensive business litigation that lasted almost two years. I had never expected that I would ever find myself involved in a lawsuit. I also could have never imagined how emotionally draining it would be and how it had nothing to do with facts or real business. It has everything to do with emotions and feelings, like a nasty divorce. As the lawsuit was resolving, I met a wonderful and inspiring woman, Stacy. Three months after meeting her, I dropped my lucrative job, rented out my house on Capitol Hill (that I had only purchased eight months prior), accepted a job with one-third of my current pay and moved to Los Angeles to join a start-up. The move also allowed me to live closer to my father and stepmother who had also recently moved to Los Angeles. I believed in Stacy, wanted to be part of what she was doing and to be near my father. I also needed a break from the emotional trauma of the last two years and felt that a move and a different professional industry would feel like a new start and give me a break from the environment that surrounded the lawsuit.

This was my first experience working with a start-up. I knew the stats on start-ups and that most of them fail within the first five years. To be safe, I continued working as an independent consultant for my former employer in a limited capacity. I would spend a couple hours in the evenings and work on the weekends providing consulting services. Because we were in start-up mode, Stacy and I were roommates. Los Angeles is an expensive place to live, and we were both making sacrifices on pay. We were excited and had a fun and cool place to live in Westwood. When I started working full time with my new company, it became obvious there were problems with the business plan and serious problems with the work environment. I felt confident the company would fail. And, I witnessed the slow deterioration of Stacey s spirit. She was suffering from an abusive work environment caused by the same CEO she had hired to run her own company. He convinced the other founder to slowly push Stacy out of the day-to-day operations and bullied her in meetings. Stacy got up early every morning and had breakfast, consisting of tomato soup and sardines. She would get out two little appetizer plates and share her sardines with my two dogs, Senshi and Rambo. Then, one morning Stacy didn t get out of bed.

4LNS is the name of my company. The morning Stacy didn t get out of bed was the day I started 4LNS. Over seven months, I had watched Stacy s life at work deteriorate under bad leadership, and I had seen her spirit slowly get crushed by a bully. When Stacy didn t get out of bed, my dog Senshi, was lying outside her door with her nose stuffed in the crack between the door and floor sniffing her out. I knocked on Stacy s door and asked her if she was coming downstairs for breakfast. She didn t want to get out of bed. I told her that I loved her and that Senshi loved her too. I told her was worried about her and asked her if she could hear Senshi sniffing and looking for her. Stacy said that it wasn t because she was loved; it was because she could only offer sardines. When I simply responded that it was for love and sardines, she got out of bed and joined us for breakfast.

Experiencing the sadness and dimming of Stacy s beautiful and bright spirit made me reflect on who I was and what I stood for. I told her I would be resigning that day from her company and encouraged her to leave it behind also. I went into work, resigned and told the CEO why. I couldn t be part of a company that was not aligned with what I stood for, my purpose and how I believed people should be treated. I came home, opened the legal zoom website and started 4LNS, for love and sardines," later that afternoon. My company, 4LNS, would be a reflection of myself, would always be accountable to my values, standards and my truth. My leadership and business approach reflects what I stand for, how I want people to know me (my purpose), how I take care of myself, how I treat others and how I contribute to the world. Daily I bounce my actions and decisions off my stand, my purpose and my intentions. This formula has served me and has allowed me to build a beautiful company that I am proud of while also maintaining an equally beautiful and balanced life:

Tell everyone what you stand for. I stand for people with privilege mobilizing their influence and power to remove obstacles and clear a path for others to realize all of life s opportunities.

I think it s important to tell people my stand because I m proud of it. I tell my business partners what I stand for and cultivate my stand with intention when I interact with my partners and the members of my 4LNS team, my family, my friends and my community. I align myself and my company with partnerships that reinforce my stand. This is how living my stand works with a business partner. My company does the majority of its work in the defense industry and generally would be referred to as a federal or defense contracting company. I have a very small company in this space and currently do about 3.8 million gross a year and have 15 employees. My main business partner does about 2.7 billion a year and employs more than 20,000 people in 60 different countries. I ll call them XYZ. The first work I got for my company was with XYZ because I asked. When I asked, I aligned my request to what I stand for. Right after I started 4LNS, I called the senior executive of the XYZ, another Veteran. I told him I needed his and his company s support to add my company as a full subcontractor to the Navy effort we were both supporting. This would allow me to begin building critical past performance for my company and would strengthen our partnership. I asked for his support and influence within his company to open opportunities for me, and I knew that he had the power to advocate for 4LNS within XYZ. I also had the insight and trust with his Navy client to ensure that, as a team, we were doing our best work to be able to increase our manpower on the contract.

As a giant company and a micro company, we both have the power and privilege to clear obstacles and open paths for each other. Over the past six years of partnership, we have done that. It hasn't always been completely smooth, but by voicing my stand repeatedly, it gave us something to anchor our partnership. Now I feel like the senior management of our teams operate seamlessly, and this management relationship transfers to our employees working on site, as well as provides excellent support to our customers. When I meet with other companies that are potential partners, my stand is where I start. I share with them the purpose and the values I'm outlining in this chapter, and I give them examples of how I will treat them as a partner and how I want to be treated. Then, I ask them to share the same with me. I do not work with companies that do not share my values. There is no opportunity or amount of profit that would make me waver from this principle.

Your purpose is your life s job description. My purpose is to be an indestructible force leading people to realize a full life.

I am unwavering in my commitment to build the best life and opportunities for my 4LNS team and partners. The components I focus on are fearless communication, balanced life and clear paths to opportunity. Fearless communication starts with trust. If there isn t trust in your relationships, there is no future for them. As applied to work, I must be able to voice my concerns, problems and mistakes with my business partners without fear. My team must be able to talk to me without fear of reprisal. I have to be able to have difficult conversations with my team without concern for the health of my company.

For example, the most prevalent and worst use of fear-based leadership I have seen used in the defense industry is during a contract re-competition. I have both experienced this as an employee and talked to people who are victims of it in their workplace. There are legal limits to the lengths and ceilings of federally awarded contracts. When contracts begin getting close to term or ceiling, the federal government will often reopen those contracts to competition to broaden the opportunity for competitor companies to increase the value of the performance or decrease the cost of services. Obviously, the incumbent contractor team performing the work has an advantage of insight on the requirements of the job and the people performing the work under contract. When contracts are about to expire, competitor companies begin head-hunting incumbent employees and asking for their resumes to submit as part of their proposal for the new contract award. Often, incumbent companies threaten their employees with termination if they find out any of them have supplied their resume to a competitor company. I have been on contracts where an incumbent has lost the work, and they have threatened employees with legal action if they accepted a job with the winning team. This means that this company would rather their employees lose the job they have worked for the past five years, a job that company no longer can offer, than go to work for the winning team. I want my team to choose not to provide their resume and knowledge to other companies because they believe in 4LNS, and they want us to have the best advantage to win, not because they are scared that I am going to fire them or take legal action against them.

Most companies require employees to sign nondisclosures and noncompete clauses in their employee agreements and then use fear-based leadership tactics to try to get their employees to follow them. I don t include non-disclosures and noncompete clauses in my employment agreements. Recently, one of my contracts was reopened for competition. I educated my team on the competition process, how we as a team could put our best foot forward to win and the potential outcome. I told them that companies might contact them and ask them for information and may ask for copies of their resumes and sign letters of intent. If they chose to do that, I would take no action against them. But they care about our team, and I knew by the end of our conversation that no one would take advantage of an offer. Fear can also be used by employees against their employers. I have recently began working with a non-profit organization that had a cadre of employees that openly threatened their senior management with destruction of IT infrastructure, smearing of reputation, malicious information sent directly to the board of directors and mutiny if things did not run the way they thought they should. This went on for over a decade and over time degraded the organization to a point that it almost had to close its doors.

For decades the term work-life balance has been the buzz. Generally defined it is the amount of time you spend doing your job compared with the amount of time you spend with your family and doing things you enjoy. The acceptance of that kind of approach to work and life makes me cringe. I have a problem at 4LNS if my team isn t enjoying their job because that means 4LNS team members don t have a full life, which is counter to my life s purpose. A full life is a balanced life, but the balance isn t work and play." It s a full balance, not separated into components and it feels really good when you achieve it. Think about when you are at a restaurant, and you first sit at the table and it starts moving around because the floor or legs are different heights. The first thing you do is grab a sugar packet or fold up your paper napkins and stick them under the legs to stabilize and balance the table. Trying to have a meal on a table that is clanging around is not enjoyable. For me, work is just one leg of that table, like spending time with loved ones, taking care of myself and serving my community. I want my work life to be a great and balanced part of my full life.

I also want this for my 4LNS team, and I try my best to ensure I foster an environment that gives my team the opportunity to balance their lives. An example of one way I do this at 4LNS is by providing them a flexible work environment. I give my team the option to work from any environment that they find to be most productive. I have office space available to them if they want to come to an office or I allow them to work from home full time or I provide a mixture. I know that it is difficult for some leaders to let go of the direct oversight approach to their employees, but I keep my focus on work product. I know good from bad. Just like you would not have to actually see furniture being built to be able to tell the difference between the furniture in my house made by a craftsperson from the twenty-five-dollar particle board shelf I bought off Amazon and put together myself. If I have a team member who isnt performing, but is trying, I spend time with him or her to better align the job requirements until we can find where he or she thrives. This is not always easy. I have spent years working with a good, dedicated employee before we figured out how he thrives. I also know every industry doesn t have the ability to offer a flexible work environment or tailor a job to every individual. My suggestion would be to explore ways to offer flexibility and as many options as possible within the work environment to increase happiness at work.

It is my responsibility to ensure that I remove any obstacles and reinforce all paths that lead to bigger and better opportunities for my team at 4LNS. A traditional approach of providing upward positional mobility is not available at my current size and operating structure because I run my entire company without any overhead positions. I focus on building responsibilities/experiences and certifications into my employees resumes, so they are competitive for other jobs even if they aren t with 4LNS. I provide the mentorship and resources for individuals to do business development in order create a new opportunity and job for them within 4LNS. And, I provide the mentorship and resources for individuals to start and have their own company if they want to go down the path to entrepreneurship or start working for me after they have already started. These are approaches that have proven successful for me. I have found additional gig work for three of my employees who have their own separate businesses, and I am on the verge of starting a new line of business thanks to the passion of one of my team.

Set your daily intentions.

1. Give your self" a spirit name. I am The Shining Heart."

I am intentional about taking care of my self." There are many resources on self-care, and I recommend taking advantage of them and making self" intentional every day. My approach is to incorporate visualization into my process of self-care. Visualization is the process of creating a mental image or intention of what you want to happen or feel in reality. An athlete can use this technique to "intend" an outcome of a race or training session or simply to rest in a relaxed feeling of calm and well-being. Michael Phelps is well known for utilizing visualization. Military Special Forces also use visualization techniques, such as emergency conditioning or battle proofing. The Shining Heart" is how I feel when I ve optimized care for my body, mind and spirit. I radiate warmth, light, love and health from my heart chakra.

In 2019, the failure rate of startups was around 90%. Research concludes 21.5% of startups fail in the first year, 30% in the second year, 50% in the fifth year and 70% in their 10th year. In two more years, 4LNS will make it to the ten-year mark. I do enjoy running 4LNS. However, it is also challenging and stressful, I work very long hours, and I can never truly take a vacation. There is a lot of pressure and also moments of frustration and defeat. The Shining Heart" is how I manage the stress of entrepreneurship and keep work as a good part of my life. I also encourage the rest of my 4LNS team to concentrate on self-care.

2. Define the wake of your path through life. I am a super-power mirror.

I believe our paths create a wake as we move through life, like the wave pattern of a moving object through water. I am intentional about how the wake of my life impacts others. I am a superpower mirror. When people interact with me, I want to make them aware of their own superpower. I always want to reflect their best qualities back to them, and I hope that ripples to the next person they touch as they move along their path through life. In my company, I reinforce the superpowers of my team collectively and individually. I also use this approach with my clients and partners. When I treat others this way, I have found that I am also treated with appreciation, trust and respect of my personal and the 4LNS superpowers. Who doesn t want to be part of the superhero club?

3. Be of service.

4LNS is a reflection of me. I believe in service. It is important to me to volunteer my time to support my community. My focus areas are women and veterans, and I also apply the principle of service to 4LNS. My company donates financially to multiple organizations, and we offer in-kind support in software development, branding and marketing to multiple veteran service organizations.

Acknowledgement

I feel grateful to Mark Mhley, my friend and Naval Academy classmate, for inviting me to write a chapter of this book and the other veteran contributors for including me in the effort. Thank you to my Aunt Max for helping me, she is a brilliant and talented editor and writer. I dedicate my chapter to the memory of my father Harvey Fernebok and my basketball coach Warren Crutchfield. I believe that the best way to honor the memory of someone you love is to serve your community with good deeds, and I try my best to do that every day.

Harvey Fernebok, Alyce Fernebok and Ginger
Summer 1979

Harvey Fernebok and Alyce Fernebok, Marine Corps Ball
November 1996

Coach Warren Crutchfield and Alyce Fernebok
August 2017

Alyce Fernebok
Captain, USMC
linkedin.com/in/alyce-fernebok-a06414b

CHAPTER THREE

Bobby Brown

I am early in my transition out of the military. My decision to retire, confidence to aspire to something new and the thought of what to do following my retirement was based on the lessons I learned as a child, my imagination, and the Benjamin Franklin quote I have adopted as my mantra: If better is possible, then good is not enough." If you are reading this during your transition, you are about to embark on another journey where you will be tested. I recommend that you imagine your success before you start. Imagination is key because if you cannot imagine success you will never dream about it and therefore, you will never achieve it because you will not work to attain it.

As a young child, I spent the summers of my formative years at my grandmothers home in White Hall, Alabama. White Hall, a former sharecropper community, located in Lowndes County is also known as Bloody Lowndes County" after its dark history of death and lynching of blacks by racists and Ku Klux Klansmen during reconstruction and the Jim Crow era. Highway 80, which is now famous as the track that Civil rights marchers took during the 1965 Selma-to-Montgomery Civil Rights march, borders White Hall. As a child in the 1980 s White Hall lacked resources and still had dirt roads. We would have to drive Highway 80 to Montgomery for groceries and other various appointments. During those drives, my grandma, parents and other relatives would tell us stories of how things used to be during the 1960s and earlier. Highway 80 provided me a front-row seat to a painful history and created a foundation for the life lessons that I would apply to my personal and professional decisions.

My grandmother is a strong, church-going woman and I recall her working as a domestic for most of my time growing up. Although she did not march from Selma-to-Montgomery, she said she got into what the late Georgia Congressman John Lewis called, Good Trouble" by participating in a lot of other civil rights and voters rights demonstrations. Her involvement in other demonstrations was dangerous and often presented challenges for them in maintaining their property and therefore their livelihood. Along those lines, they taught us some very important qualities that I have brought with me throughout my life. They taught us to put God first in all things, to keep our word, to take advantage of opportunities presented, and the value of hard work.

In 7th grade, I visited the Naval Academy on a class bus trip from Mobile, Alabama—where I lived— to the DC, Maryland, Virginia (DMV) area. During our visit to the DMV, I was fortunate enough to stop over in Annapolis, MD. That day we visited the State Capital grounds and the United States Naval

Academy (USNA). The visit to USNA would change my life because it increased the limits of my imagination of what was possible. I believe that you can only dream about the things that you can imagine.

We toured USNA and I got to witness a noon meal formation in Tecumseh court or T Court" as they called it. There seemed to be thousands of midshipmen going through their daily routine of mustering and marching into King Hall for lunch. I remember seeing the crisp white uniforms and swords and I wanted to be a part of that special environment. I did not see many black midshipmen or other midshipmen of color, but I did not care, I wanted to be a part of the grandeur and military pomp and circumstance which was happening before my eyes.

Once I got home, I told my parents I wanted to attend USNA. My dad said, Okay, how do you think we get you there?" I remembered our family saying A dream without work is only a waste of time." I knew that meant that I was going to have to do something to accomplish my goals and make my own dreams come true.

I considered myself to be from a middle-class family, mainly because my parents were able to meet our basic needs. My mom worked swing shift for 30+ years at a paper mill and my father was a mortician.

Eventually, my parents divorced, and my father remarried and started another family. I was the oldest of five in a blended family. If my parents, like their parents, did not work, they did not get paid. We learned through their examples, the value of hard work. We also learned that regardless of how hard you work, you must have someone open doors to opportunities for you to be successful.

After applying to 8 universities, I finally received my nomination and appointment to USNA. There was just one twist, I had to attend the Naval Academy Preparatory School (NAPS) in Newport, RI for a year beforehand. I did not understand why I had to attend NAPS – a foundational program – for a year before being admitted. After all, I was accepted to Notre Dame, Purdue University, The University of Alabama, Tulane University, and Morehouse College as well as a few other top-named universities.

Equipped with a belief in God, core values, and an understanding that nothing would be given to me, I left Mobile, AL for Newport, RI. I remember the day I left Mobile and I promised myself that I would not fail out of the Academy and return home. I felt like even though I wanted to attend USNA, I had the added weight of representing my family and everything they had endured in the south to afford me the opportunity to attend a service academy.

I hated Newport when I was there for NAPS. NAPS indoctrination numbed me to being homesick, but when I was in uniform, I felt I was special. However, exploring the North East was a cultural adjustment, but it did not take long for me to be reminded that I was a black, 18-year-old male in an affluent seafaring town. I earned a steady income, was challenged academically and formed life-long friendships. Looking back on it, that year went by fast but while I was there it felt like an eternity. I completed NAPS and earned another nomination and was appointed to attend USNA.

The mission statement of the Naval Academy begins with To develop midshipmen morally, mentally, and physically......." Not only did they develop me, they challenged me in those areas also. After a slow start, I finished the Academy. I was in the middle of the pack academically, a varsity football letterman, and a Battalion Commander. Most importantly I earned a pilot slot after commissioning. Times were challenging for me during my time at the Academy. I constantly reminded myself that I was representing something larger than myself and that I was a sharecropper s grandson, attending the best higher learning institution in the world. While it may have beeen a big challenge, failure was not an option. I wasn t going back home.

Once I landed at the Academy, my family values were formalized and I adopted synonyms for the values I learned from my grandmother and parents in Alabama.

Do right" became—"Live with honor"

Work hard" became—"Be dedicated"

Know who you are and from whence you came" became—"Be a leader with integrity".

I earned my first pick for service assignment following graduation—Naval Aviation. The academy challenged me morally, mentally, and physically. It was a leadership laboratory and I had an opportunity to develop and truly understand that to be a good leader, you must be a great follower. I also learned that other than my own individual preparation and hard work, two of the largest indicators of success are mentorship and advocacy. Your ability to network and provide or receive mentorship from that network is critical to your success. Advocacy is even more important. I learned that you must have people to open doors and give you opportunities to perform.

I entered the fleet as a newly winged Naval Aviator and flew the SH-60B helicopter. I earned my call sign-*Downtown* - during my first operational flying tour in Mayport, Florida. I was fortunate that it would follow me through other operational flying tours to Hawaii, and ultimately through my Command tour at Helicopter Maritime Strike Squadron FOUR NINE (HSM-49) *Scorpions* in San Diego, CA.

After 20 plus years as a Naval Aviator, I decided to retire. I thought back on about year ten, the first time I thought about leaving the Navy. I was going to resign from my commission and go into the private sector. After a conversation with my father, and to his urging, I decided to stay and retire for the benefits. I do not regret staying in, but I think you must recognize that you can become institutionalized and comfortable. While you are in the military, you generally do not worry about how you will provide for your family. Family sacrifices and difficult career choices may be presented but you know that you will be compensated twice a month. An Aviators career path is generally mapped out for you and as long as you perform, follow the path, you should move up the ranks—it s all laid out for you. You learn quickly when you re considering retirement, that you ve become a jack of all trades, but a master of none as it compares to civilian careers unless you are going to continue to fly. The career differentiators are the educational and non-operational opportunities that you capitalize on.

During a conversation with my wife—who is an entrepreneur—I quickly realized that if I was going to transition from the military, I needed to expand my network beyond my military circle. I had to start picking up business and entrepreneur mentors and gaining exposure to all the possibilities that would be awaiting me during my transition. If you are seeking transition advice mainly from active duty personnel, you need a new network.

I wanted the personal challenge of defining my own path, and I knew I could be successful in another space, while continuing to serve. I knew it would be tough, but it felt right. So, when I began my transition—which I am still working on to this day—I had to see what else was out there. I m still charting my path. I had to figure out my passion and purpose. My passion is to create purposeful opportunities in business that provide financial security and allow for quality time for my family. I know who I am and still feel the pressure to succeed based on my personal journey.

My military transition back to civilian life was like when I was 18 deciding to attend USNA; however, this time, I was making a decision for a family with the pressures of providing for my family. The best advice I can give is that if you can t figure out the one thing (job or entrepreneurial effort) you want, it may be more important to find what you don t want to do. Knowing what you don t want may lead you to determine an 80% solution, what you don t mind doing. Hopefully what you do not mind doing will provide the appropriate purpose and compensation to support yourself, your family and your accustomed lifestyle. The biggest difference with your decision at this stage of your life is that you have the freedom to do and become whatever you want.

The same rules apply, you must work and it s helpful to find mentors and advocates for support.

I had a meeting with a mentor before I began my transition, who is an executive of a large consulting firm. He looked at my resume and told me that while I had super-hero status, I did cool stuff, led in challenging spaces in the military, had over 2500 hours of flying, that he had no idea where to place me. My skillset was not easily transferable to command the compensation that I was expecting. Understand, the Civilian sector will appreciate your story and respect you for your service; however, if you are trying to break out of defense, often times, they have no idea where to place you. A lot depends on their timing and whether or not they need an immediate impact player in the position because you probably have all of the soft skills required, but you may present a gap for them in the hard skills necessary to fill the position. The most important thing to remember is that your timeline may not line up with their opportunity to bring you on. Be patient, and continue to put yourself out there, because something WILL happen. Remember too, that words are just words until you have a signed offer letter or contract, and even then, some things can change.

I recommend you ask yourself, where and how can you add value to your civilian job or your entrepreneurial pursuit. Once you map out your value proposition, truly dedicate yourself to working harder than ever, and leaning on your network for mentorship and advocacy and you will be ready for your transition. Understand, there are a lot of good guys and gals having a hard time transitioning because they are not adding value to whatever they are doing.

When you re used to a certain way of living, it can be a challenge to change, but you must determine your purpose and carve out a space to figure out what you love. If you get stuck because you can t figure out what you want to do, my 80% solution is to find out what you don t mind doing and make sure you get compensated for it. So that s where I started, but I ended up in a much happier space. I have a great job with an amazing company that provides my family with a great standard of living—all the while, I m dabbling in entrepreneurial endeavors.

Transitioning out of the military is an emotional roller coaster. It will sometimes make you question who you are, what s your role, and whether you are making the right decision. If you considered yourself to have super-hero-status" you may begin questioning your abilities when you hear No" or don t get a response for the first time from a prospective employer. After all, all your *military friends* said you were great, and you thought you would probably not have a problem getting a great job when you retired. What do they know? They have not transitioned out of the military. Your emotions are natural. Unfortunately, there are service members who are overwhelmed by those emotions and change in status and decide to commit suicide. It s devastating, but it doesn t have to happen. I encourage you to get counseling or connect with other transitioning veterans for support. It s ok that it takes time to adjust to the change in status from a military leader to a civilian. There are so many other veterans that will talk with you and are willing to help you. Don t be afraid to ask for help. Even better, we veterans further along must be engaged and not be afraid to approach those in transition and take the time to help them. It s up to us to help support even if it s just connecting them to resources or networking.

Veterans, if you choose, will continue to be a key network for you long after you decide to transition. I am still able to connect with a veteran community through my volunteer work and business ventures. I serve on several non-profit boards that support veterans transition and focus on veteran homelessness, substance abuse, and mental illness. There are opportunities to engage with veteran networks if you desire.

There are a lot of great veteran business resources that can be shared, like Re4ormed, Mark Mhley s company. I ve found it is a great resource for connecting veteran entrepreneurs. Your local

Chamber of Commerce is also a be helpful for promoting your business.

The amazing group of authors that I join in this book are a part of the family as well. Lionel Hines and I played football at the Academy, and Alyse Fernebok and I knew of each other at the Academy, but our paths continue to cross in the San Diego area while serving on boards and volunteering.

We are all human and share the same anxieties when it comes to change and transition. The only difference is our perspective and how we respond to that change. My transition to the civilian sector created an opportunity for me to reflect on the different stages of my life. I thought it was helpful for me to reflect on the conditions from whence I was raised for strength and confidence. I leaned on the lessons that I learned in the Navy and when things were uncomfortable and challenges were presented, I leaned into my network for guidance and mentorship. One of the biggest adjustments I had to make was to increase the talent available within my network. I recognized my fears, uncertainties and sought out support and that helped me realize that I was not alone. Increasing the talent within my network allowed me to imagine the possibilities of a new reality. Now that I am about two years into my transition, I am working to fulfill my purpose. I am thankful for my wife and daughter s patience and support during my transition. Figure out your purpose and work to fulfill it.

Bobby E. Brown, Jr.
Commander, USN, Retired
www.linkedin.com/in/bobby-e-brown

CHAPTER FOUR

Brian Rivera

It s About Flow

Everybody has a plan until they get punched in the mouth. -Mike Tyson

West Seattle Garage Band of Brothers

In a West Seattle row house garage, a small band of brothers armed with Post-it notes, Sharpies and a wall full of flip chart paper applied a Red Teaming technique to rapidly share out ideas on naming a company and developing its core product. What emerged was AGLX, the company name, and High-Performance Teaming™, AGLX's product or service. A few days later, with some help from LegalZoom, I officially became a veteran entrepreneur.

At the time of this garage gathering, I was immersed in the Seattle Agile scene, working as a full-time employee at Alaska Airlines as a Scrum Master. In the four years that had passed since leaving active duty service, I held an equal number of jobs, including a stint as a government service employee, a brief stop at Amazon, and some time as a 1099—a gig employee with a military-themed consultancy. In my spare time, I read books on cognitive science, neuroscience, complexity, the science of teams, high-reliability theory, human factors, and anything that could help me understand human and organizational performance. To show the world I was employable, I packed my resume and LinkedIn profile full of three- and four-letter certifications reminiscent of military acronym soup.

During this immersive period in Seattle, I realized that the leadership and teamwork lessons we applied at the tactical level of fighter aviation created the *group flow* or the *optimal team experience* that leaning-forward organizations and teams were trying to achieve through modern business practices. However, the problem with modern business practices is that they fail to address the human factor—the DNA common in all organizations.

The creation of AGLX and High-Performance Teaming™ was a defining moment, a moment when I decided to codify the leadership and teamwork experiences that I learned in the U.S. Navy and apply them to helping business leaders create the agility, safety, resilience, and innovation their companies need to survive and thrive in this volatile, uncertain, complex, and ambiguous (VUCA) world. But as legendary boxer Mike Tyson eloquently points out, "Everyone has a plan until they get punched in the mouth."

The metaphorical punch to my entrepreneurial mouth did not come as a single shot. Instead, it was the accumulation of multiple low-impact body blows from software teams, coaches, and business leaders who pushed back on the idea that agility was an outcome of interactions or teamwork skills. From my military experience, I knew that agility, not Agile, required that teamwork skills be learned, practiced, and reinforced at all levels of the organization. What made these body blows unusually painful was that the majority of concepts, methods, and frameworks behind Agile had military origins.

What is Agile?

I am still searching for a better way to answer that question but, to be fair, it is a set of principles and values often used by and associated with software developers. Agile, as I learned it from some of its thought leaders, has military origins and is about delivering value early and often to customers.

My unfiltered view of Agile is described as this:

Agile is a pseudo-science lined echo chamber where it is not uncommon to find socially awkward people attempting to coach other socially awkward people social skills.

This may be a bit harsh and dramatic, but this is how I see it. And make no mistake, in the eyes of those who have not served, veterans are often perceived as awkward – difficult to deal with and lacking critical "business" skills. As an entrepreneur, I set out to change these paradigms.

Search the web for top ten skills, skills of the future, or any combination of "skills" and "future work" and you may come across results from LinkedIn, the World Economic Forum, and other reputable business management organizations. Search results will include skills such as *decision making, assertiveness, planning and learning, leadership, communication, adaptability, dealing with complexity and ambiguity, situational and self-awareness, coaching, leveraging cognitive diversity,* and *overcoming biases.*

All these future skills are non-technical or soft skills in nature; they are the leadership and teamwork skills that we set out to target with AGLX's High-Performance Teaming™. HPT, as we called it, combined the non-linear decision-making activity known as the OODA loop with the five principles of High-Reliability Organizing and the teamwork lessons found in the U.S. Navy's Crew Resource Management program—the foundation of team science.

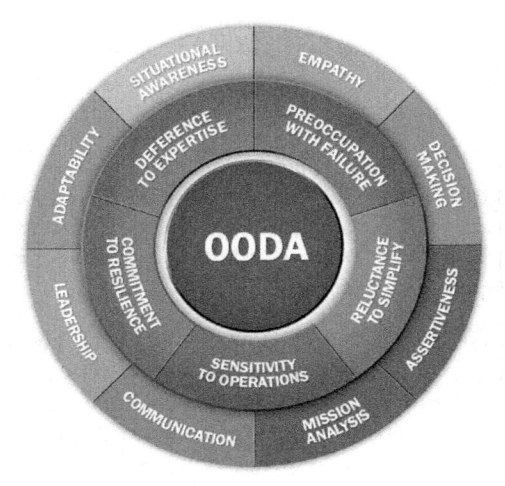

Figure 1: AGLX's High-Performance Teaming Model

In theory, AGLX's HPT had the solutions to 80% of organizational problems. In reality, the insular military optics projected by AGLX and High-Performance Teaming™ combined with common human biases, to include belief perseverance, allowed decision makers and the Agile community to easily reject our offerings. As a result, AGLX failed to get airborne.

Then COVID-19 happened.

A week before the global 2020 COVID-19 lockdown, I took to the TEDx stage in Budapest, Hungary and delivered my talk, *Design for Flow*. The talk was on the topic of human and organizational performance and borrows from physics, psychology, and *The Flow System*™—a system of understanding that helps individuals, organizations, and governments survive and thrive in the age of complexity. And that's exactly what COVID-19 revealed: the age of complexity.

Almost overnight, AGLX went from garage band to a global brand. Through Steve McCrone, a former New Zealand Defense Force serviceman, AGLX stood up an Asia Pacific office and we are currently sorting out details for expansion in Europe. In the organizations we coach and train, "Agile" is being replaced with High-Performance Teaming™.

The book, *The Flow System: The Evolution of Agile and Lean Thinking in the Age of Complexity,* which I co-authored with a former Toyota executive, and a team science and complexity professor from the University of North Texas, became a Forbes-noted "Top Mind-Opening Business Book for 2020." Additionally, leadership development and MBA programs around the world are including The Flow System™ in their curricula.

> Key Message:
> To match and even outpace the acceleration of future work trends triggered by COVID-19, entrepreneurs and leaders must embrace complexity thinking, teamwork, and leadership lessons known to and lived by many veterans or risk the rapid demise of not only their company, product, or team, but their own future employability.

The journey I want to share here is more about *we* than *me*, a recognition of those people who helped shape my thinking and contributed to the growth of AGLX and the creation of The Flow System™. For veterans in transition and future and current veteran entrepreneurs, the two takeaways I want to impart with you are: (1) the power of the veteran network and (2) the need to step outside of that network to create new pathways not only for you, but for other veterans. For business leaders interested in thriving in our post-pandemic world, my story will help you understand why hiring veterans is imperative while providing insights on how to survive and thrive in this VUCA world.

Finally, I'm going to share and connect some ideas on what I call *Future Flow,* a global well-being effort led by a network of veterans who are tackling veteran suicide, PTSD, TBI, anxiety, and depression through the use of natural sciences—the same sciences that inform High-Performance Teaming™ and The Flow System™.

Context: That Time I Was Almost a Government Entrepreneur...

"Any foreign innovation in a corporation will stimulate the corporate immune system to create antibodies that destroy it."
-Peter Drucker

The Department of Defense's (DoD) culture is a threat to national security, this according to organizational psychologist and Wharton professor, Adam Grant who spoke to the U.S. Senate Armed Service Committee in early 2021 on management challenges within the DoD. From my experience and Adam Grant's testimony, the DoD is a bureaucratic system where rigid hierarchies, egos, and pages of protocols, processes and policies create a culture of complacency and conformity to the status quo. In short, the DoD is no place for mavericks or entrepreneurs: creativity and innovation is destroyed by the DoD immune system.

My entrepreneurial story starts when I became a DoD Government Service (GS) employee. Although not a typical or recommended path for becoming an entrepreneur, this pathway offered me the least resistance given my situation: a separating service member living overseas. To be clear, I was not retiring, I was separating at the 16-year mark of active duty service, four years short of qualifying for a lifetime pension.

Situation Report. I had no product, service, or company to be considered a current or future entrepreneur. I had plenty of in-demand skills relevant inside the DoD. I was living in Germany with my wife and our two little girls. We needed income.

Course of Action (1): I could gamble with a fixed, future separation date from the U.S. Navy and hope that a state-side hiring manager outside my network would extend a job offer to me that coincided or overlapped with this fixed date.

Course of Action (2): I could apply for a GS job that paid the bills and gave me the flexibility to leave at my leisure while I continued to develop my professional skills and search for a job.

My wife and I chose COA 2, but this came with a risk.

Nearly fifty percent of the GS workforce within the DoD are veterans. Why? The work is familiar, job security is high, and the pay is fair. In fact, voluntary turnover in the federal government is less than 7% whereas voluntary turnover in the industry is around 30%. By choosing COA 2, I ran the risk of becoming part of the system, a system that crushes the entrepreneurial spirit. Fortunately, with the help of veteran networks and within 18 months of accepting a GS role, I would be included in the seven percent.

I share this story not to bash government employees—I know that systems drive behaviors—but to build some context and identify the period when I realized the strength of the veteran network, in and out of the government.

Laminar Flow: My Military to Civilian Transition Part I

My flight path to becoming an entrepreneur was full of laminar and turbulent flow, not to mention a few in-flight income emergencies, some self-induced. The laminar flow or smooth flow I experienced during my transition and entrepreneurial journey occurred when I engaged or worked with other veterans.

For example, my GS job search was made easy by several veteran-to-GS websites, veteran hiring preferences, and the support of several GS employees in my U.S. Africa Command office who were veterans themselves. With all this help, and a 25-page USAJOBS resume, I ended up with 13 interviews. The canned questions were easy to answer, and I ended up getting several offers including one for a role in the very office I was currently serving in uniform. I went from Lieutenant Commander Rivera to Mr. Rivera almost overnight.

With my basic needs satisfied by my GS role, I continued to leverage and build my veteran network to find meaningful work outside of the DoD. On one occasion, in the summer of 2013, I contacted a former squadron mate, Kevin "Catfish" Sidenstricker, who proudly displayed the acronym "CSM" on his LinkedIn profile. Out of curiosity I called "Catfish" to ask him about the CSM acronym and his job search experience.

"Catfish" shared with me that employers were looking for people who held a Certified Scrum Master (CSM) credential. According to "Catfish," the pay was great, and that as a former naval aviator, I already knew everything Scrum had to offer. He also pointed out that in the eyes of many hiring managers, the two-day and 35 question Scrum certification carries more weight than actual experience on any high-performing team. So, I signed up for a CSM course in Frankfurt, Germany and began my Scrum journey.

Scrum, for those of you who are not familiar, is a team framework used to solve complex problems and is inspired by the OODA loop of fighter aviation and the Toyota Production System. For my naval aviation brothers and sisters out there, Scrum is TOPGUN's Plan-Brief-Execute-Debrief (PBED) cycle meets Total Quality Leadership. I would learn much of this from the co-creator of Scrum and former RF-4C fighter pilot, Jeff Sutherland, PhD when we met in person.

I made contact with Dr. Sutherland through LinkedIn and we agreed to meet in Amsterdam, Netherlands in January of 2014. In Amsterdam, Dr. Sutherland talked about the origins of Scrum, its connection to the OODA loop of fighter aviation, and he suggested that I should start a consultancy of former aviators who "go around and stomp out all the bad Scrum and Agile in industry." I had no idea what he was talking about at the time, but I nodded my head to this new direction of travel, friendship, and opportunity.

LinkedIn became a powerful tool that allowed me to connect directly with veterans and hiring managers in the companies that I wanted to work for, to include Amazon, Apple, Google, and some financial services companies. I also used LinkedIn to participate in various Scrum and Agile groups where I would blog about the origins of Scrum, its connections to Mission Command and the OODA loop, and why aviators make the best Scrum Masters and Agile coaches. One of my blogs about the connection between TOPGUN's PBED and Scrum caught the attention of former F-15C fighter pilot James "Murph" Murphy, the founder and CEO of Afterburner, Inc., a military-themed management consultancy whose content is built around TOPGUN's PBED cycle.

After a couple of phone calls, "Murph" invited me to visit his company in his Atlanta, GA headquarters. After passing what is arguably the toughest interview in the world, "Murph" extended an offer for a full-time position. I accepted, flew back to Germany, submitted my GS resignation letter, and began preparations to move from Germany to Atlanta, GA.

Hedge, TOPGUN Style
In 2010, a few years before my transition, I found an online advertisement for Fox Three Options, now Top Gun Options.

This online options class offered by a former F/A-18 TOPGUN Adversary pilot, E. Matt Buckley, call sign "Whiz", would influence how I thought about the value of veterans' skills and experiences applied to complex systems. To date, this class is the second most important training and education I received in my life. The first: life in fighter aviation.

To most people, options are dangerous, come with risk, and are for professionals who manage money. "Whiz" dispelled this thinking as he applied lessons from fighter aviation to help individual investors make sense of the market, learn various options tactics, and build a risk management orientation through hedging—protecting or limiting the risk of any adverse event.

Hedging is exactly what every entrepreneur, leader, and team needs to know how to do to succeed in this turbulent world. In fighter aviation, we always planned for contingencies, those situations that were not favorable to achieving the mission but were likely to happen given what we knew about our internal and external operating environment. During my transition and entrepreneurial journey, hedging (aka optionality) is what put food on the table, shelter over our heads, and created new opportunities.

Turbulent Flow: My Military to Civilian Transition Part II

With our household goods shipment en route from Germany to Atlanta, GA I had to make a destination change as the full-time position with "Murph" and Afterburner, Inc. turned into a 1099 role. I had to find other employment, fast. Fortunately, as a hedge, I continued to interview with Amazon and a small Seattle area stock brokerage for "Agile project management" roles.

Following a series of interviews, I received an offer from Amazon and was rejected by the small stock brokerage as I lacked "real" Agile Coaching experience.

The veteran network at Amazon was fantastic, but for some reason, much like the financial services company and the small stock brokerage, I could not convince the various Amazon hiring panels that my military service and education translated into knowing how to lead and be part of a high-performing team—the very skills behind why Afterburner, Inc. hired me. At Amazon, I did not get the job I wanted at Amazon, I got the one I needed: a management role in one of Amazon's newest fulfillment centers (FC) south of Seattle, WA.

Within the first year of employment, all Amazon employees must attend a one-week leader orientation course that explores flow and lean concepts, company values, and Amazon's leadership principles. Central to this course is Jeff Bezos' 1997 letter to shareholders—a letter that is studied by entrepreneurs and leaders who are interested in understanding the value of customer obsession. For me, this leadership course in Arizona was my first stop on my road to becoming an Amazonian and would later influence High-Performance Teaming™ and the most critical aspect of The Flow System: Customer 1st Value Delivery.

One of the first five people to interview me at Amazon was also attending the leader orientation course[1]. He remembered me, was shocked that I did not get an Agile PM role, and arranged for me to join his product team in Seattle as an Agile PM; but to do this, I would need to interview in Seattle and get an endorsement from my FC general manager.

---

[1] Manish, his first name, would go on to be a successful founder and CEO of an advanced supply chain and logistics company

On a short break from my Amazon FC training now in California, I flew up to Seattle to do some house hunting and visit Amazon's headquarters to interview for this new Agile PM role. On my walk from my downtown Seattle hotel to the Amazon campus, I took a phone call from the hiring manager of the small stock brokerage who earlier passed on me for a role as an Agile Coach. Greg Myers, the hiring manager, was calling me from Seattle to let me know a new role opened up and wanted to know if I was still interested in the job. I told Greg I was in Seattle and I could meet later that day.

That afternoon I accepted the offer from Greg and the small stock brokerage. Just an hour later, I was offered the new Amazon Program Manager role. Given a choice, I preferred to stay at Amazon, but that decision was now in the hands of an Amazon fulfillment center general manager.

When I returned to California to continue my Amazon training, my general manager asked to see me immediately to discuss the situation. He denied my request to change roles within Amazon. I tried to convince him that I wanted the transfer, but he simply said something to the effect of, "You were hired for and accepted this role, I will not approve this transfer." He went on to say, "Unless you have another outside job offer, you are stuck with me for a year."

That was my last day at Amazon. I was hedged.

Building Strength: Learning from and Helping Others
If you don't know, you'd better ask somebody

GySgt. Irving Anderson, USMC
OCS Class 13-96 Drill Instructor

Greg Myers and his team welcomed me to the Seattle-based stock brokerage, a former startup that was now part of the same financial services company that I initially interviewed with in

Plano, Texas. As I settled into coaching software teams, I started to realize what Jeff Sutherland told me a few months earlier about the amount of bad Scrum and Agile out there.

At work, I was surrounded by several good coaches and two great mentors, Ashok P. Singh and Greg Myers. Ashok challenged me to publish articles and speak at different Agile and Lean Meetups around the Seattle area. He also encouraged me to apply to speak at regional and global Scrum Gatherings on the topics of teamwork and high reliability theory. I credit Ashok's feedback and constant encouragement for helping me become a better speaker and in making the decision to start AGLX.

When Greg Myers shared with me the Theosophical statement, "When the student is ready, the teacher will appear," I think he was letting me know it was time for me to open a new pathway: the pathway where a mentee seeks a mentor. As a mentor, Greg spent hours with me, asking me questions and sharing new concepts and techniques such as how to mitigate cognitive biases and the power of sense-making in organizations. In fact, it was Greg who introduced me to liberating structures (found in Red Teaming) and the Cynefin framework; both would have a profound impact on High-Performance Teaming™ and The Flow System™.

As I was performing well in my role, Greg asked me if I knew anyone else with a similar background who may be interested in filling an upcoming coaching role. I knew a few people including future West Seattle Garage Band of Brother and former squadron mate, Chris "Deuce" Alexander. Not only did I help "Deuce" land his first job out of the military as an Agile Coach, but I also started to help other veterans learn how to move directly from wearing a uniform to coaching Agile teams. I took that turbulent flow I faced during my transition and made it into laminar flow for others, creating new pathways for veterans to find meaningful employment including another

West Seattle Garage Band of Brothers and veteran, Ryan Bromenschenkel.

In this "gig" economy, it isn't unusual for full-time employees to have a side job or jobs to make extra cash. For me, Afterburner, Inc. was that side gig and gave me an opportunity to be around other high performers, including former Navy SEALs, naval aviators and the occasional tolerable U.S. Air Force officer who mistakenly joined the wrong service.

Like Amazon, new employees and 1099s of the military-themed company, Afterburner, Inc., had to attend indoctrination to include some in-depth training. My trainer happened to be E. Matt Buckley call sign "Whiz," the same "Whiz" who four years earlier taught me options trading using lessons from fighter aviation. In Atlanta, "Whiz" showed me and a handful of new clients how to apply TOPGUN's Plan-Brief-Execute-Debrief cycle to help companies deal with the turbulence associated with rapid changes in technology, increasing competition, and changing customer preferences.

On the road with "Whiz," "Murph," and other top veteran entrepreneurs and consultants, I facilitated various workshops for clients' sales, operations, and logistics teams and helped executives work through new strategy and product development. All of this non-technical skills work was familiar to me as it was burned into muscle memory from my time in the cockpit and at the operational and strategic level of warfare.

One year into my Agile immersion in Seattle and the gig work with Afterburner, I realized that companies don't need a set of principles and values to create agility. They need to learn how to lead and work in teams throughout the organization.

Appreciation: Hive Mind & "Charm School"
A hive mind has been used to describe high-performing teams in sports, the military and emergency medical services. The

term, hive mind, is another way to describe when people stop acting like individuals and start operating as one or a single entity. If you have ever been a member of a high-performing team, you know what it is like to have a hive mind, you know what it is like to experience group flow.

Flow, according to psychologist Mihaly Csikszentmihalyi, is when a person or group is in a state of optimal experience, when nothing else seems to matter. To achieve group flow, several triggers must work together to help drive a team's attention to the present moment. These triggers include a shared understanding of the goal or direction of travel, good communication, rapid feedback, concentration, a sense of control, shared risk, close listening, and the blending of egos. Additionally, high consequences along with some volatility, uncertainty, complexity, and ambiguity in the environment help drive a team to flow.

For me, I first experienced group flow as the lead trumpet in an award-winning high school jazz band and as a member of a nationally recognized jazz ensemble. In the U.S. Navy, I would rediscover this optimal experience in combat, large scale training exercises, and as an F-14 instructor, to include coaching new pilots how to land on an aircraft carrier at night. But the ultimate flow came when max-performing the F-14 in front of millions of people during airshows.

As a member of the F-14 Tomcat Demonstration Team—a collateral duty only available to less than 1% of naval aviators—we shared grave risk to self and others and had all the triggers necessary to drive attention to the present. Flow was guaranteed. But flow isn't something that just happens.

In naval aviation, we didn't rise to the occasion, we sank to our level of training. And it is our training, not the technical training of how to employ the aircraft, but our training on how to work together as teams that allowed us to achieve group flow.

Additionally, our agility, safety, and resilience were emergent properties of our teamwork skills, not a dogmatic belief in a set of principles and values posted on our ready room bulkheads. In fighter aviation we didn't "Do Agile" and we certainly didn't "Do Safety." Instead, we focused on building high-performing teams. We called those teams "crews."

In his wildly successful 2015 book, *Team of Teams*, Gen Stanley McChrystal has a chapter dedicated to the secret sauce behind building high-performance teams. That secret: aviation's "Charm School." In naval aviation, we didn't call it "Charm School," we knew it as DAMCLAS—an acronym for decision making, assertiveness, mission analysis, communication, leadership, adaptability, and situational awareness—the components of teamwork.

DAMCLAS is part of naval aviation's Crew Resource Management (CRM) training program, a program that borrows and is modified from commercial aviation's CRM program. Commercial aviation's CRM program came about when aircraft accident investigators started to see a trend in the 1970s and '80s where roughly 80% of aircraft accidents were caused by human factors or poor leadership and teamwork skills, not technical malfunctions.

All naval aviators learn DAMCLAS skills and are held accountable for sustaining these soft skills during each event of TOPGUN's Plan-Brief-Execute-Debrief cycle with an emphasis on the most important event, the debrief. It is in the debrief where naval aviators look back at what happened, understand how things happened and dive into the causal factors as to why those things went the way they did. Through effective debriefing, which requires knowing how to work as a team first, individuals and teams improve their situational awareness or sense-making capabilities which in turn helps them notice more in future execution. And it is the ability to notice or appreciate more (being present) that ultimately creates flow.

Probe: Find Out What Works

Taking the Meetup stage at Seattle's Museum of Flight with Dr. Dan Low[2], an Assistant Professor of Anesthesiology at the University of Washington and an anesthesiologist at Seattle Children's Hospital, to discuss the similarities between F-14 crews and surgical teams to a group of software developers and Agile coaches may seem like a good way to waste your evening. But this Meetup sponsored by AGLX would provide us invaluable feedback on whether or not a market existed for what we offered with High-Performance Teaming™.

At the time of this Meetup, I had moved on from the small stock brokerage to a full-time position at Alaska Airlines as the company's first Scrum Master. Dave McCormick, a U.S. Army veteran and head of Product Management and Portfolio Delivery for Alaska Airlines, offered me a full-time job following a teamwork, debrief, and agility talk I delivered to the Seattle-based airline's information technology division.

While working at Alaska Airlines, I connected the company's Crew Resource Management and Threat and Error Management pilot trainers to its software teams and demonstrated that teamwork lessons from the cockpit can be applied to software developers. At the University of Washington and Seattle Children's Hospital, Dr. Low did essentially the same thing: he applied lessons from the cockpit

---

[2] Dr. Low attended a multi-week Toyota Production System course in Japan as U.S. hospitals were fixated on adopting principles of Lean to improve safety and efficiency. But early in his career as a Helicopter Emergency Medical Services (HEMS) crewmember, Dr. Low was exposed to human factors or CRM training by a former British SAS helicopter pilot.

to one of the most complex environments in the world, surgical teams.

On stage, Dr. Low shared with the Meetup crowd that the third leading cause of death in the United States is connected to the poor teamwork and leadership skills in our health care system. He also provided data and anecdotal evidence of the power non-technical (teamwork) skills training has on improving patient safety. Behind the stage, Dr. Low invited me to see for myself, a visit to watch surgical teams in action at Seattle Children's Hospital. What I witnessed reminded me of the teamwork skills we used in the cockpit.

Not long after this meetup and hospital tour, I left Alaska Airlines to become an underpaid and over-traveled Agile coach. This time at another financial services company, traveling from Seattle to the East Coast, and from Seattle to California to coach the mortgage division that many pundits claim was behind the 2008 housing crisis—this experience and irony is worth a whole book on its own.

What I saw in this role was that the financial services company's culture was a threat to their own survival. Much like the DoD, this company had a bureaucratic system full of rigid hierarchies, strong egos, and pages of protocols, processes, and policies. To make things worse, the company was spending money on consultants who delivered on frameworks, not teamwork. I used the opportunity to learn, apply activities from High-Performance Teaming™ when I could, and accepted that I was hired to help them "Do Agile" and not create conditions for flow.

To take advantage of the long travel times and time away from home, I read books by former options trader, Nassim Nicholas Taleb to include *Antifragile*, *The Black Swan*, and *Fooled by Randomness*. I studied Russel L. Ackoff and his work on systems dynamics. I became fascinated with Daniel

Kahneman's *Thinking, Fast and Slow* and Peter Senge's *The Fifth Discipline*. I read Gary Klein's work on decision-making, books on teamwork and psychological safety by Eduardo Salas, Scott Tannenbaum, and Amy C. Edmondson. I read books on high reliability theory by Karl Weick and Kathleen Sutcliffe, books on safety by Rhona Flin and Sidney Dekker, and the list goes on.

My two key takeaways from all of this reading: (1) the common thread among the market, the brain, teams, and organizations is that they are all complex adaptive systems; and (2) they are also flow systems, ever evolving systems that exist to provide better access to the currents (money, blood, information, value, etc.) that flow through them. These takeaways combined with my experience in the military and as a consultant led me back to two foundational frameworks.

The first was the sense-making framework Greg Myers shared with me in Seattle, the Cynefin framework. The other framework was the non-linear decision-making process often associated with fighter aviation, Col. John Boyd's OODA loop. So, I went deeper.

Sense-Decide-Act

As we know, there are known knowns; there are things we know we know. We also know there are known unknowns; that is to say we know there are some things we do not know. But there are also unknown unknowns—the ones we don't know we don't know.
-The Honorable Donald Rumsfeld

When the Secretary of Defense (SECDEF), Donald Rumsfeld, dropped the above word salad on our 2005-2006 Air Command and Staff College class of mid-grade officers, I initially thought he had lost his mind. But this wasn't the case. Our SECDEF was not losing his cognitive faculties, he was repeating what he learned from Dave Snowden, the creator of the Cynefin framework. Ten years would pass before I would learn about this Cynefin-to-Rumsfeld word salad connection from Dave Snowden himself.

During a four-day Cynefin Masterclass held the week of the 2016 Presidential election in San Jose, CA, I met Dave Snowden and I quickly learned that a five-minute conversation with Dave requires four hours of additional reading and research. Dave's connection to SECDEF Rumsfeld was through some 9/11 work he was doing for DARPA on a human terrain mapping program known as GENOA II. This military program, according to Dave Snowden, would further the development of the theory that surrounded his Cynefin framework.

At its core, Cynefin is a sense-making framework, a way for leaders to understand the nature of their present environment—clear, complicated, complex, chaotic or confused—so they can apply the correct response. The Cynefin framework is a meta-framework that can be applied to any context from a start-up to the hedge fund, from Agile to the Oval Office, and safety to 5th Generation or Liminal warfare.

My military background and familiarity with fundamental ideas and concepts such as Mission Command, crews, High Reliability Organizing, and human factors (all found in High-Performance Teaming™) helped me connect with Dave Snowden. In the classroom, Dave Snowden leverages these ideas and concepts to help leaders understand how to use his framework.

Over the past several years, I spent a lot of time with Dave either participating in his workshops or retreats, speaking at various global conferences with him, and even co-leading workshops at Toyota, NATO, and the OODA loop-Cynefin exploratory held in Quantico, Virginia, the home of John Boyd's archives.

John Boyd's Observe-Orient-Decide-Act (OODA) loop and Dave Snowden's Cynefin framework complement each other and have a shared heritage in complex adaptive systems and non-linear decision making. During the OODA-Cynefin exploratory, in addition to Dave Snowden, I was fortunate to bring in two mentors, both military veterans, who previously helped me develop a deeper understanding of the OODA loop, retired U.S. Army and Marine Don Vandergriff and retired USAF Col. Dr. Chet Richards.

Don is a great mentor whose expertise is in Mission Command and in what is known as outcome-based learning (OBL)—a 21st century adult learning approach that focuses on developing critical thinking and leadership skills fit for complex environments. Don's work has been accepted as the official learning doctrine of the U.S. Marine Corps in its 2020 Learning Strategy and Campaign plans. He is also an expert in Boyd's OODA loop and maneuver warfare and often collaborates with Dr. Chet Richards, one of John Boyd "acolytes."

Not long after I met Dave Snowden, I connected with Dr. Chet Richards through LinkedIn and asked him for some of his time to discuss his work on the OODA loop and that of a former Dutch F-16 pilot, Dr. Frans P.B. Osinga. On several Zoom calls, Dr. Richards and I dove into the OODA loop and Boyd's interest in complex adaptive systems thinking as well as Dr. Richard's book, *Certain to Win: The Strategy of John Boyd, Applied to Business.* One of the topics that Dr. Richards loved to talk about was John Boyd's fascination with the Toyota Production System (TPS) and how many early *lean* thinkers didn't truly understand the philosophy and practices of Taiichi Ohno, the father of the TPS. Interestingly, a few weeks after one of my last Zoom calls with Dr. Richards, I was offered a coaching role at Toyota, working for Jeff Sutherland, the co-creator of Scrum. My post-military apprenticeship journey had come full circle.

Working for Jeff Sutherland was incredible as I was surrounded by top coaches and trainers to include Nigel Thurlow, a TPS and Agile expert. I stayed with Jeff Sutherland's Scrum, Inc. for a while including a tour at the oil and gas services company in Houston, TX. During this tour, I decided to move my family from Seattle, WA to Virginia Beach, VA—what I consider to be the nexus of modern military and business teamwork practices.

This move put me closer to Washington, D.C., where I would spend my weekdays when I voluntarily left my high-paying consulting job with Scrum, Inc. to put on a uniform and support my U.S. Navy family hurting from two high-profile mishaps at sea.

17

In 2017, seventeen U.S. Navy sailors were killed in two separate collisions with commercial vessels during routine operations. The causal factors behind these collisions were no different than the causal factors behind the majority of aircraft mishaps, the third leading cause of death, and why organizations, products, projects fail in industry. When the Secretary of the Navy asked for reservists with consulting backgrounds to join a small team that would be responsible for identifying Industry "Best' Practices on culture, safety, teamwork, and leading indicators, I jumped at the chance.

The report our team produced, *Industry Best Practices & Learning Culture –The Competitive Advantage of a Learning Culture,* included input from the majority of my mentors and many of the academic authors I previously mentioned. Unfortunately, the DoD's immune system pushed back on what I consider to be the two most important frameworks for dealing with complexity: Dave Snowden's Cynefin framework and John Boyd's OODA loop. Also missing from the report were Mission Command, Red Teaming, and Wardley Maps.

Although I was a little disappointed with the final product, the insights in the document are sufficient enough to help budding entrepreneurs and military leaders set up teams and start their journey on creating a winning culture.

While on this team, my three key takeaways from engaging with top business leaders and academics were: (1) the origins of team science are in the U.S. Navy's Crew Resource Management and Tactical Decision Making Under Stress Programs; (2) industry "Best" Practices are borrowed from the military or are derivates of military concepts; and (3) there are too many consultancies thriving off of pseudo-science.

Fire Together, Wire Together

There is an axiom in neuroscience that describes how pathways in the brain are formed: "Neurons that fire together, wire together." Like neurons connecting in the brain, friendships and ideas are all about timing.

Serendipity brought Professor John Turner to Nigel Thurlow's front door. John Turner thought it would be a good idea to meet the couple whose dog sitting want ad was answered by John's mother. During this quick front-porch meeting, Nigel discovered that John was a team science and complexity professor at the University of North Texas. The rest, as they say, is history.

I met John during one of the Navy team engagements where Nigel and his Toyota Connected team, and Major Max Gerome and members of the Dallas Police Department sat together to discuss the similarities between software development and policing. Nigel, who I met when working with Jeff Sutherland, had become Toyota's Chief of Agile at Toyota Connected.

Following my stint with the Navy team, Nigel asked me to work for him at Toyota to include delivering AGLX's High-Performance Teaming™ workshops to software developers.

Mark "FUN" Mhley, one of the veteran entrepreneurs in this book, co-facilitated these workshops.

Nigel had a clever idea to bring the three of us together. John Turner, Nigel Thurlow and I met together over a weekend to see what would emerge. Much like the Seattle Garage Band of Brothers that met a few years earlier, the three of us were armed with Post-it notes, Sharpies, and were Red Team ready. With our attention on to the present, our egos blended, and feedback loops unobstructed, we found flow and created The Flow System™.

What emerged from Thurlow's dining room was the Triple Helix of Flow, the DNA of Organizations: Complexity Thinking, Distributed Leadership, and Team Science. We added a customer 1st focus and as our foundation the Toyota Production System and The Toyota Way. We created a system of understanding that can be applied to options trading, digital transformation, warfare, Agile, Lean, safety, or anywhere humans interact with other humans and technology.

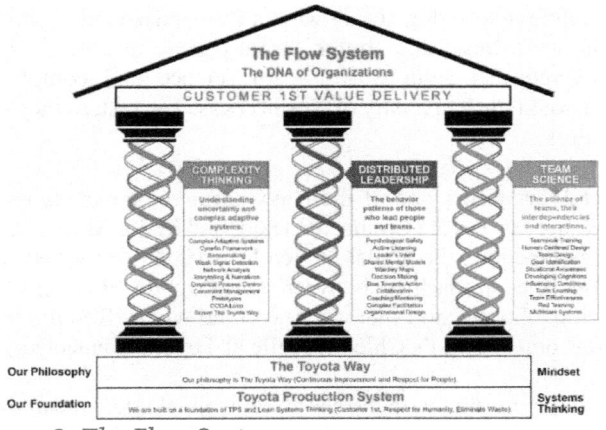

Figure 2: The Flow System

As of this writing, The Flow System™ Guide has been translated into 18 languages, an MBA program that features The Flow System™ will be launched later this year, book sales are strong, and The Flow Consortium has launched an online accreditation program.

For me, seven years after leaving active duty, my entrepreneurial journey is only beginning.

Future Flow: Make 22 equal to 0
Since 9/11, the number of service members and veterans that have died by suicide is four times greater than those killed in combat. Estimates suggest that every 65 minutes a service member or veteran loses an often unseen internal battle to suicide. We need to turn 22, the total daily number of service members and veterans who commit suicide, into 0.

Why am I bringing this up in a book about veteran entrepreneurs?

Our well-being, not just veterans, but the mental health and happiness of our friends, families and co-workers is deteriorating as a result of the stresses associated with the acceleration of technology, emerging global threats, and uncertainty in our post-pandemic world. Just as the awareness of the scalable solutions to creating group flow, and organizational agility, safety, and resilience have come from veterans and the networks they create, so will the naturalistic solutions to treating post-traumatic stress disorder (PTSD), traumatic brain injury (TBI), depression, anxiety, addiction, and more.

One of my key insights from developing High-Performance Teaming™ and The Flow System™ is that inside mirrors the outside. Our brains are complex adaptive systems where the quality of connections matter, just as the quality of interactions within a team matter more than the quality of each team member. When those connections or interactions are broken or weak, we are not whole, we cannot achieve flow.

To repair those broken or weak connections in the brain caused by PTSD, TBI, or other stressors, many veterans are turning to psychedelics. I'm not talking about the recreational use of the Schedule-1 drugs but the medically supervised use of naturally occurring psychoactive substances found in plants and animals such as ibogaine, 5-MeO-DMT, ayahuasca, and psilocybin. From my basic understanding of the science, psychedelics create new connections between neurons by increasing the density of dendritic spines—small protrusions that aid in the transmission of information from neuron to neuron—and stimulate synapse formation. In layman's terms, psychedelics help neurons fire together so they can wire together. It's about flow.

From the veterans I know who have gone through treatment, the results have been nothing less than astonishing: in as little as a weekend, veterans are reporting their addictions are broken, anxiety is gone, and some no longer meet the diagnostic criteria of having PTSD. As a co-creator of The Flow System™ and veteran entrepreneur who is diagnosed with PTSD, it is my honor to donate my share of proceeds from this book to two non-profit organizations that are leading the charge in turning 22 into 0: Veterans Exploring Treatment Solutions (VETS) and the TOPGUN Fighter Foundation (TGFF).

To learn more about the awe-inspiring work VETS and TGFF are doing, visit their websites at https://vetsolutions.org and https://TOPGUNfighterfoundation.org

To learn more about AGLX, High-Performance Teaming™ and The Flow System™, visit www.aglx.com, https://flowguides.org, and https://www.getflowtrained.com

Brian Ponch" Rivera is the co-creator of The Flow System™, founder and CEO of AGLX Consulting, co-founder and co-owner of AGLX Holdings, and a founding member of The Flow Consortium.

Ponch," his callsign from naval aviation, is a first-generation college graduate and earned his commission through Officer Candidate School. He served on active duty for 16 years before transferring to the Navy Reserve and now wears the rank of Captain (O-6) as a part-time member of the Defense Innovation Unit.

As an entrepreneur, Ponch" leverages the leadership, teamwork, and complexity thinking lessons he learned throughout his diverse military career to help individuals and organizations create the agility, resilience, and safety they need to survive and thrive in this turbulent world.

Ponch" lives in Virginia Beach, Virginia with his wife, Allison and two daughters, Carmen and Camille.

Brian "Ponch" Rivera
Captain, USNR
AGLX Consulting: https://www.aglx.com/
Flow Training: https://www.getflowtrained.com/
The Flow System Guide: https://flowguides.org/

CHAPTER FIVE

Craig & Mark Hodder

A Father and Son in Service

It is not unheard of to find families with generations of service members. Living in, growing up around and being a part of a military family instills a certain passion and pride for the country. Mark Hodder and his son Craig are no exception. Both father and son served our country, and continue to serve veterans in many ways today—despite both being retired from the military.

Mark Hodder

Mark Hodder, an Officer s Candidate School (OCS) graduate of 1964 opted not to accept a commission and went into the reserves as a corporal for three years before deciding to become an active duty officer. From 1966 to 1969, he served our country as a Marine Officer and spent 13 months in Vietnam as a naval gunfire spotter and forward observer. In 1969, he retired from the Marine Corps as a Captain and went to work for Naval Academy graduates and Harvard MBA s. Mark said, I loved the practice, but I hated the game. It changes a lot of things when they start shooting at you."

After leaving Vietnam, Mark was sent directly to temporary duty in Puerto Rico for six weeks and didn t have the same distasteful welcome that other soldiers coming home from Vietnam had. He didn t have to deal with any of it, but without a shadow of doubt, Mark wouldn t have let it affect him anyway. His attitude in regard to the non-welcome, was simply that he didn t care what they thought. He knew what they d been through, what they d survived, and opinions didn t matter to him. Being in Puerto Rico, working as a range control officer, he spent his free time swimming, being in the sun and enjoying the beautiful scenery. It was meant to have a six week shelf life, but Mark loved it so much, he stayed for an entire year!

For Mark, the camaraderie of the brothers and sisters in service with him was incredible. Being attached to an artillery battery and being one of the few Naval Gunfire Spotters in Viet Nam meant being assigned to many units for short term operations. Infantry units, other artillery units, Viet Nam Army patrols, Special Patrols, different ships, they were a few of the assignments. Not knowing it then, but looking back, this was Mark s introduction to what we now call Networking" in the business world and prepared him to be a traveling salesman.

One of the funniest stories Mark still laughs about today was when another officer there—a fire control officer—both of them the same rank, both leaving Vietnam at exactly the same time, (they went over there as part of the 5th Marine Division, which was recommissioned again after being decommissioned after WWII). Mark really wanted to go to Camp Pendleton in California and the other officer wanted to go to Camp Lejeune. They had the same rank. Both put in their requests, And in its wisdom, the Marine Corps sent us both where we didn t want to go. We just had such a good time complaining and fussing and carrying on about the wisdom of the military and how they made their decisions, and everybody in the battery thought it was the biggest joke ever that we both wanted to go to different places and could have swapped easily, but didn t get it to work out." Camaraderie was found in the scariest of times, in the depths, in the barracks, in the jokes and in the fun. It was all around and was what held the Marines together in the time they needed each other the most.

Craig Hodder, grew up knowing a bit about his dad s time in the military, but Mark didn t talk much about it. Craig had eclectic interests in high school but at one point decided he wanted to be a military pilot for the purpose of becoming an aircraft mechanic. He wanted to find his way from there to becoming an officer. Hitting the top mark on his Armed Services Vocational Aptitude Battery (ASVAB), the recruiters were trying hard to get him into the nuke program—but he wasn t interested.

Mark said that Craig is an extremely bright guy. He scored the highest ever scored on his science test in high school, but he failed the course because he didn t do his homework. They had to really figure out what to do with him because he was a AAA student, in terms of tests and class participation, but when it came to handing in his homework, he just didn t want to do it. He s very independent like that. I m not going to say that he was anti-authority, but he questioned authority terrifically. When he came to his mother and me and said he was going to join the Navy, of the 300 things we thought he might do, that wasn t even on the list.

When Craig graduated high-school, Mark bought a boat and together they towed it across the United States from Florida to California. Our objective was to hit every BBQ place we could hit on the I-10. We had a ball—we just had so much fun. At the end of that trip, I was taking him to boot camp in San Diego, and I can t speak for other veterans on how they feel about their family, but I didn t quite understand how much my dad must have gone through while I was in Vietnam until I drove up to the boot camp and saw a big sign there that said, The Thunder and Lightning of Desert Storm Starts Here . That was something. From that time on, I just really appreciated what my dad had gone through." The pride of a father when watching his son on his own journey is something that is truly immeasurable.

It was in the 1980s that Mark had started a business, MLH Services—a print and graphic design service for brochures, flyers, business cards, postcards, donation envelopes, certificates, etc for businesses and entrepreneurs—and through that business, created a lot of connections with veterans. After Craig s separation from the Navy in 1996, he came to work with his dad in the family business. Mark said, After Craig spent 6 years in the Navy, I had already started my businesses in 1980. When he got out of the Navy, I asked him what he wanted to do, and he said, I d like to come to work for you." I said, Okay." We needed some real help in computers, and Craig needed to learn every aspect of the business. It was really his choice to come into the business and I loved it. I always thought it was terrific having him close and watching him grow and become a business man. I was really pleased with him. Now, of course, I ve given the reigns over to him, so there is a path of succession." Mark is so proud of the longevity in which he and his son have worked together in business. After 20-25 years together, his favorite thing is watching his son grow into a top-notch executive. Mark gives some credit to the Navy for helping to shape him into a man of service, one who is customer centric, sensitive to those that work for him and with him, and into an incredible leader. Of course, knowledge and experience have helped as well.

Craig Hodder

After enlisting in the Navy and graduating from boot camp, I became an Avionics Technician and rose to the rank of E-5 (Petty Officer Second Class). After 6 years of service from 1990 to 1996, I left the Navy.

During my time in the military, I spent a great deal of time doing Temporary Assigned Duties (TAD), which wasn t what I was trained for, nor what I wanted to be doing. It was what ultimately guided my decision to separate from the Navy.

Make no mistake from what I ve told you, and I tell anyone this that asks, I loved the military. I loved being in the military, I loved the people I worked with—but I despised the people I worked for. It s a difficult thing for some people to understand, but the best way I can describe it is with my second command in Miramar. Our commanding officer and our XO were marvelous. They were interested in all of their members, even if they were just the guys that sanded and painted the airplanes. They were interested, they were engaged, and they were always willing to talk to us. They didn t stand apart. Meanwhile, the folks who were involved in the nitty gritty, they were not nearly the personable sort. The ones who ran the operation—gave the orders—were the ones who made life difficult. Way more difficult than it needed to be. The people I worked with, were my friends. I still have connections to some of them.

One of my closest friends went all the way through the 20 years in service before he retired, and we ve been in touch the whole time. The short answer, it was definitely a brotherhood, but it was stratified. The brotherhood didn t appear in a flash, not for me, it evolved. It was a day by day progression that developed the family feel for me. Over time, with different events, that s how I learned that these men and women that I worked with were my comrades."

For folks with my experience that didn t have that war-time" experience—the high adrenaline, do or die, life and death experience—it was more what I would call organic. I learned who I could depend on, and who I couldn t over time. We had events" like losing a fighter pilot to a crash, but we didn t have that galvanizing quality like being in a foxhole while people are shooting at you type of event that would solidify that brotherhood instantaneously.

Some of the individuals that I had been in service with became friends in the military and we never really stopped being in connection afterward. Whether that was phone calls or letters, we stayed in touch. A decade or so later, there were a few happy accidents that brought me back in contact with my brothers and sisters from the military. Social media helped me to find a lot of my military comrades once it became a widely used internet option. Unlike relationships in person—in civilian life—it has been my experience that relationships that existed when we were both on the aircraft carrier together, 15 years later in getting together for dinner, it is almost like pushing pause on a VHS tape. Everything just sat there and waited for you to get back to it. It was like no time had passed. You sit down to dinner, and it s like someone hit play, and you re laughing, joking and smoking just like it was 15 years ago. The relationship just didn t change one bit.

As a veteran, connection with other veterans usually starts with me noticing something about them. For example, my company does a lot of customer service, and I ll be on the phone providing customer service to someone and they ll use the phonetic alphabet to spell out the bits that are important. It s a dead giveaway to me that they are veterans, or they had family in the military. No one uses the phonetic alphabet quite that way. We will usually share a laugh and then an instant connection is made. There s a common language there, even if we didn t serve together, we understand each other without a civilian ice breaker—it s already built in."

The Veterans Business Network

The unspoken family dynamic that is built by serving together is something that sticks with the men and women in the military, long after they leave the military. All of the veterans involved in this anthology are part of groups, businesses, and/or programs that help veterans transition and thrive in one way or another. One of these businesses, The Veterans Business Network (VBN) serves a number of the authors in this anthology.

Over 30 years ago, Mark and Steve White—a fellow author in this anthology—started the Veteran s Business Network (VBN)—where they work with veteran business owners looking to build, branch out, and create more revenue and impact. Through the VBN, Mark and Steve believe that veteran entrepreneurs are stronger and can do things like hire veterans, contribute to their community, assist wounded warrior programs, and help combat mental health issues and PTSD. The VBN does this by providing opportunities for networking amongst veterans. They find veterans in business and set up events where they can network with each other, meet each other, exchange business cards, and create business opportunities. When they create more opportunities, it helps them make enough money so that it is available for them to turn around and help more veterans succeed.

One important belief that Mark and Craig share is that helping veterans doesn t just come from throwing a check at a charity. Helping veterans comes in many ways, Mark said, The most important thing to me is a recognition from the top of the government all the way down to the smallest entrepreneur. That veteran businesses are important. What they do is important, what they foster is important, and with an estimated 2.5 million veteran businesses, they are just really important to this country. The thing that is most important to me is making sure that all of those veterans that have served come out with something to do that has an impact on the country, the economy, and our way of life. If I can help with that, my spiritual gift is giving, so it s something I ll do forever."

Craig said, I don t feel that sending money off to a veteran support organization is supporting veterans". I would rather do the work for organizations like The Honor Bell nonprofit that provides honors for fallen veterans that otherwise may not receive them, or buy $1000 worth of food and take it to a food bank that serves veterans rather than just giving money to a random organization. To me, it feels more like expressing support. It is not a bad thing to contribute to these organizations, but given the choice to write a check to a place or taking food to the VFW, I d rather see the physical support for veterans than cut a check to an organization that may or may not actually support our brothers and sisters and their families." It is about the intrinsic value and extrinsic value combined.

Both men, while having different experiences in the military, take pride in their service, respect and love their country and continue to be a driving force in the support of their fellow brother s and sister s pursuit of the American dream.

Mark L Hodder
Captain, USMC, Purple Heart
MLH Services LLC/ Veterans Business Network
www.mlh-services.com
mlhodder@mlh-services.com
https://www.linkedin.com/company/35442486/admin/

Craig Hodder was born in 1972 and raised at many points up and down the East Coast. When he was a Senior in High School in Florida, he chose to join the United States Navy as an Enlisted Aviation Electronics Technician (AT), hoping to work on the F-14 Tomcat. He joined under the Advanced First Term program, and entered the service after his schools as a qualified AT attached to Fighter Squadron ONE FIFTY FOUR the Black Knight flying F-14 Tomcats in Atsugi, Japan. He served with this squadron on board the USS INDEPENDENCE, taking part in Operation DESERT STORM, before being transferred to Fighter Squadron TWO ONE THREE the Black Lions in Miramar, California. Leaving the Navy in 1996, he returned home and joined the business his father

Mark had started in 1984 – MLH Services. As part of a family business, it was his duty to learn every aspect of the company. His time in the military was invaluable in this regard, and after many evolutions of himself and the business, he now is the CEO of MLH Services. MLH Services is the sole sponsor of the Veterans Business Network – also started by Mark Hodder – a Veteran Community service organization dedicated to the advancement of veteran business-to-business networking.

Craig Hodder
Second Class Petty Officer, USN
CEO, MLH Services
www.mlh-services.com

CHAPTER SIX

Craig Washburn

We all have our own reasons behind our decision to join the military and serve our country. I had multiple decision points come together that made the path a clear and easy choice for me. When I was young, I made a deal with my parents that I would pay for half of my college education. The idea was my father's because he made the same commitment to his parents. We both agreed that I would value my education more if I was involved in it financially. I began saving and spent multiple summers during high school trying to prepare financially to meet that obligation. From waiting tables to cleaning pools, I worked hard to be ready.

I started college in Tallahassee, Florida the first available semester out of high school. Unfortunately, I was there without a vehicle, so I was riding a bicycle everywhere I went. I knew the only way I could keep my end of the bargain was I needed to work part time while attending school. I applied at any and every job I could think of within biking distance. The problem was Tallahassee is home to both Florida State University as well as a community college and competition was tough. To my dismay, I could not find a job. I quickly found myself running out of money. Honestly, it didn't take long. As I was getting toward the end of the semester, realizing that I was out of cash flow for the next semester, I had to decide to either go home and live with mom and dad and attend a community college there, or to—as I put it—man up and try to find a way to fund college on my own.

As the stars aligned, things were heating up in Kuwait at the very same time. It was right before the first Gulf War. I had been watching what was happening on TV and I felt a call to action building inside of me. The path became clear—I was going into the military and was going to be a part of whatever was coming, and I was going to be able to put some money away for school. Of course, my girlfriend and college friends did not like my decision one bit and thought I was nuts. I, however, was confident in my path and I knew it was the right one. Now all I had to do was figure out which branch.

I had family in both the U.S. Air Force and U.S. Army, so they were my first considerations. I then looked at the U.S. Marines and U.S. Navy. I found things in each branch that appealed to me, so the decision wasn't easy. After research and deliberation, I was ready. I ended up choosing the U.S. Navy primarily because I grew up in Florida around the water. I was certified as a scuba diver at the age of 12 and spent most of my free time on the weekends surfing and playing volleyball. I knew the one branch that would guarantee I was close to the water was the Navy so I hitched a ride to the local recruiting office and began the process. A few weeks later, I raised my hand and swore my oath to protect this nation against all enemies, both foreign and domestic.

I credit that decision as a catalyst moment because it really changed the trajectory throughout the rest of my life. Like most people growing up, going through their teenage years, and trying to figure out what in the hell you wanted to do with yourself, it was challenging. Without a lot of forced direction, sometimes when you're making those decisions on your own it can be difficult. Throughout high school, I was blessed with intellect but the public school system I was in really wasn't challenging for me, and I didn't apply myself the way that I should or could have.

When I made the decision that I wasn't going to go back home and instead, went into the military, I told myself, "Okay, I'm no longer tied to Mom and Dad. Now I need to be responsible for myself. From this point forward I'm going to put everything I have into everything I do." I went into the military with that mantra. No matter what was thrown at me, I was going to do the best that I could do at whatever I undertook. I owed it to myself and the brothers and sisters I served beside. January 3rd of 1991, I entered boot camp and started my service.

There are so many moments from my time in the military that will stick with me forever, but there are two moments that I can remember being defining. The first was in boot camp. I was about two weeks in when we were awakened and demanded out of our racks. Our Company Commander lined us all up and announced that the first Gulf War had begun and we were going to war. I still remember that day vividly. The Company Commander laid it out for us the best he could. We had barely started training, and it wasn't a drill, it wasn't training, it wasn't fake. It was time to fight for our country. We spent the morning talking through why everything we were about to learn in the coming weeks mattered. Why it may be the difference between coming home alive or draped in a flag. I remember feeling that I was part of something bigger than myself; that I was now different.

The second defining moment was during my final deployment onboard the aircraft carrier, USS SARATOGA, shortly before I left the military. We were in the Adriatic Sea tasked with enforcing the no-fly zone in Bosnia Herzegovina. The day started like most others. I was in my office below deck with my team. We kept the flight ops on the TV in our office any time they were active because we had divisions of the Weapons Department on the flight deck so we could keep an eye on what was going on. I remember looking up at the screen as an F/A-18 launched. I always enjoyed watching the planes take off. The normal path you see when they leave the catapult is the plane dips below the deck, so you can't see it for a few seconds, and then it climbs back into view. This plane, in particular, shot off the deck, dipped, and didn't climb. I immediately knew something was wrong. I watched all of the deck crew run to the rails. Without even thinking about it I ran up several decks to get to the hanger bay. Our G-5 division office sat literally right off of one of the sponsons close to the elevator. I ran to the sponson just as we were passing the plane. It had gone into the ocean. I took my boots off and was ready to jump in the water after the pilot. I got to the edge and realized at that second, that I was going to create a bigger issue for the search and rescue team than what they already had, and so I didn't jump.

That pilot, Lieutenant Scott Brubeck, lost his life that day serving his country. The fact that I was willing to put my life on the line for a pilot I never met—and will remember for the rest of my life—was a defining moment for me. It was knowing that this was my family. I knew this life, this family, would be a part of me forever.

At the end of the deployment, it was time for me to move on. I had made the decision early on that I was going to serve for four years and then go back to college. It was not because of anything that the military didn't provide me. In fact, I credit most of my success in life to what I learned while I was in the military. It was more that I started something before I went into the military—going to college—and I felt like I needed to finish that path. I also knew firsthand the toll that military life has on a family. Military life is extremely challenging not only for the service member, but also for the family. Deployments separate the family for extended periods of time. The remaining spouse has to take over both roles and navigate raising children on their own while dealing with the stress of not knowing if their loved one is coming home. Military families also are required to move to new duty stations on a regular basis. That makes it extremely difficult for military spouses to find and grow a career. It also is difficult for the children because they don't feel grounded in their schools and friends. I knew that at some point I wanted to settle down and have a wife and kids and knowing what that would mean for them, it was not a life that I wanted to put a family through personally.

When I left the military, I had a very similar mindset to a lot of the people that I served with and were close friends of mine. When it was time to go, it was time to go. It was time to get on with your life, whatever that was going to be. I think initially I left thinking, "Don't look back" but leaving your brothers, sisters and all that you've shared isn't that easy.

After leaving the military, I went back to college, then did a little time in the corporate sector, and then went back to college again. It was during my second college stent when 9/11 happened. I remember hearing the news in my car as I was driving to campus. I ran into the building that I knew had televisions in the lobby in time to see the second plane strike. As a protector, the emotions I experienced watching it unfold were overwhelming.

Like most of my Veteran friends, I felt the calling to serve again. I had one more semester that I needed to complete to graduate with my bachelor's degree, so I started looking at going back into the military with a commission. Now at 30 years old, my options were limited. After a lot of deliberation and soul searching, I ultimately decided that I was going to stay on my current path.

Fast-forward many years, I started feeling a hole that was present because I wasn't able to connect with and relate to the people that I served with. I still had lifelong friends that I'd made in the military, but life happens and you travel, and you move across the United States or the world and you lose that regular connection. I really missed the brotherhood and connection, so I started doing volunteer work for a non-profit founded by Roger Staubach, the former Dallas Cowboy quarterback and Vietnam Vet, called *Allies in Service*. They are an amazing organization and do a lot of different things, but their primary mission is to be a resource for both transitioning military as well as veterans to help them with adjusting to what comes next.

I volunteered as a mentor along with some other business leaders in the Dallas-Fort Worth area. We would have monthly meetings with the Vets. We would do trainings with them. Help them with mock interviews, resumes, you name it. That's how I got myself interjected back into the community. As soon as I got back into being around my brothers and sisters, it just felt like I was at home. What I got from, and still get from the *Allies in Service* time, is the passion for helping Vets.

During the time I was volunteering, I was also running a company that provides human resource solutions to businesses. By the grace of God, the stars aligned again. I was in a random meeting when I learned of a seven decade-plus old Department of Labor program called Veteran Tax Credits, for the very first time. It is a program that incentivizes businesses with tax credits for hiring Veterans. I was confused and frustrated because I didn't understand why, after being out of the military for 20 years, I was just learning about this program.

At first, when I was learning about it, I thought about it from a veteran's perspective. I thought, why don't I know about this? If we come with tax credits to the businesses that hire us, we can leverage that to help us get hired. I wondered how many of the Veterans I work with through Allies in Service know about this. So... I started talking to some of my veteran friends asking them what they knew about the program, and none of them knew about it. Then, I thought about it from a hiring manager's perspective because I'd hired Veterans throughout the years and left valuable dollars on the table because I didn't have any clue about this program. Finally, I thought about it from a human resource perspective. I work with businesses to solve human resource problems and they need to know about this. So...I reached out to the businesses that I served and asked them, "Hey, I know you've got vets that work for you. I placed a couple of them. How did you guys handle the tax credit?" And 95% of them had no idea what I was talking about.

I took responsibility initially—thinking I just wasn't paying attention throughout the years—but after I started talking to folks, I began to realize there was a huge delta in the education and communication around this program. I then reached out to the Department of Labor and asked them to tell me about it. They walked me through the program line by line, and I remember thinking, "Wow man, this is an amazing resource. Now tell me why, don't I know about it?" The answer I got was simple. It is a government program that is federally funded, but every state has its own team that handles it. Some states are better than others, but they are all working on limited resources and a limited budget, so they do the best they can. It was definitely an answer, but it wasn't one I liked. I dug deeper.

There was clearly a problem that needed to be solved. The advantages of this program for both the veterans and the business community were too great to walk away. Being solution oriented, I went to work to develop a platform to help veterans and the businesses they go to work for leverage this program to their advantage and solve some of the major deltas in educating both sides. After a year and a half of working with software developers, I created *VTC* –

Veteran Tax Credits https://veterantaxcredits.com. My mission is to affect veteran unemployment by getting businesses excited about hiring more veterans. It really is a win for all parties involved. The greatest reward is on a day-to-day basis, I am back working with my brothers and sisters, helping them to use this program to find work. Giving them another way to set themselves apart and shorten the transition time so they can begin their new lives. Secondarily, I am helping businesses realize those credits so they can stand up with better hiring initiatives and employ more of my brothers and sisters.

After twenty plus years out of the military, I have finally found a way to marry my two passions; being able to help my brothers and sisters as well as being able to help businesses, all within the same company. That was the drive to create VTC. It is a way to stay connected and it is a way for me to be able to meet and talk with great people on a daily/ weekly basis. Most of all, it is a way for me to give back to them so that their lives can move forward when they are ready to tackle what's next.

Looking back, it is funny how things come full circle. Obviously, the folks that I served with are scattered, so we connect when we can and usually spend an hour or two on the phone catching up. Locally, I am involved with a group of Veterans as well. I just recently moved back to Colorado but have been able to connect with them here and we meet on a regular basis to just enjoy each other's company. On a national basis, my company, *VTC – Veteran Tax Credits*, has been blessed with the opportunity to connect and partner with other Veteran-focused organizations. Together we help impact the lives of our fellow Veterans and their families.

One of those partners, friend and fellow author in this book is Mark Mhley, CEO of *Re4ormed.* When I first met with Mark and we had our first discussion, there was immediate connection and alignment. Mark is also former Navy so the stories we tell are always fun! His company, *Re4ormed,* supports small businesses that are veteran-owned or military spouse owned with solutions to help them thrive. Given that Vets hire Vets, we knew the businesses that he is working with need to capitalize on the Veteran Tax Credits because if they don't, they're walking away from valuable capital. It has been so much fun working collectively helping both veterans and businesses. We have also had great success in aligning other Veteran-focused organizations in collaborative partnerships. We know that we all have our own mountains to climb, but together we can move mountains.

It is always hard to explain to the civilian world what being a Veteran is all about. The differences in culture and the differences in vernacular just scratch the surface. It really is a different world and the experiences we share are imprinted in our DNA. I am blessed to be part of this community. We owe so much to the men and women that have sacrificed so that our Nation can live free. Join me in committing to give back for all that they have given us.

Craig Washburn is the founder and CEO of VTC Veteran Tax Credits. Craig s passion to help his fellow service members began shortly after high school. On Jan 3rd, 1991, just a month before the start of the first Gulf War, Craig joined the United States Navy. He served two years attached to Helicopter Anti-Submarine Squadron Light FOUR ZERO then two years deployed on the USS SARATOGA (CV-60). After four years of active duty, Petty Officer Second Class Washburn returned to the civilian world and completed his Bachelor of Science in Information Technology from the University of Central Florida.

Since then, Craig has held several leadership roles in the financial and insurance industries before opening his first company, in 2007. This is when Craig found another passion, helping businesses. In this role, Craig helped businesses regain control of their Human Resources budget through tailored strategic solutions. In 2016, Craig saw an opportunity to create a solution to help both Veterans and businesses better leverage a decades old Department of Labor Program, that rewards businesses for hiring Veterans. It was the perfect opportunity to marry both passions and give back to the communities that have given him so much. After two and a half years of research and development, Craig built the veteranstaxcredits.com platform and founded VTC Veteran Tax Credits. The mission of the program is to make it easier for Veterans transition into their next careers and easier for companies to generate additional revenue that can be allocated toward future Veteran hiring initiatives.

Craig Washburn
Second Class Petty Officer, USN
CEO, VTC Veteran Tax Credits
https://www.veterantaxcredits.com
https://linkedin.com/in/craig-washburn-vtc

CHAPTER SEVEN

Dan Yokoyama

While a Cadet at West Point, more formally known as the United States Military Academy, the Academy does a lot to instill the belief within you that you re amongst the best that America has to offer. The cream of the crop" as they told us many times over. In my opinion, West Point does an exceptional job of bringing in individuals who have exceptionally high expectations for themselves. Perhaps, the expectations that Cadets have for themselves eclipse the already lofty aspirations the Cadets family, Army, and Nation have for them. At least, this is my perspective, as a class of 2005 graduate from this hallowed American institution. Having exceptionally high-self expectations can be a significant motivation tool and a driver of success. However, expectations can also cut the other way, making perceived failures or setbacks even more disheartening and more difficult to deal with.

As I reflect on the past, I ve had to work on coming to terms with falling short of expectations for myself. I often feel that I was a middling Cadet who later had a mediocre carrier as an Army officer in terms of professional achievements. It s not exactly what would be expected for someone who graduates from a place like West Point. Not only did I feel that I fell short of my expectations for myself, I also felt that I let so many others down as well. You come to realize that not only does the Army expect a lot from West Point graduates, so does the rest of the country that most graduates will go on to serve. Thus, it s extremely disappointing when one feels that they have failed to rise to these expectations, and falling short can leave one with a deep sense of shame and disappointment.

At the risk of sounding cliché, I ve since realized that perceived failures do not have to define one s weaknesses but rather can be a limitless source of strength, self-belief, and grit. Those who have fallen short or failed" are also the ones who have overcome failure, whether real or perceived. The often-overlooked silver lining of failure is that the experience of failure also has the power to produce someone who is more human, self-aware, humble, and relatable to others. The lessons and education that failure can provide are perhaps the most impactful that one can experience. I ll be the first to say, that it certainly wasn t easy for me and, admittedly, sometimes I still continue to struggle with this. Yet, I also believe that nothing in this life that s truly worth it comes easy.

Everything is relative. I ll be the first to admit that I ve been very fortunate in life. I didn t grow up in a wealthy or in the perfect household, but I had people that loved me and took care of me. I didn t have to face many of the same extreme hardships as the lack of food, shelter, and a basic support structure that prevents many other young people from succeeding. Though attending West Point was a painful and often uncomfortable experience for me, I persevered. I ve also made it through three combat deployments with a total duration of about thirty months split between Iraq and Afghanistan with all of my limbs intact. I m here now and I m okay. Don t get me wrong, I know I m lucky.

However, despite all of this, I would eventually find myself in an existential crisis that lasted a period of three years or so at the tail-end of my time in the military. I knew that my military career was ending and I also knew that I would not have a choice in the matter. I knew in my gut that I would not be selected for promotion to Major (O-4). Talk about falling short of the high bar that West Point sets for its graduates. The Army was drawing down in size and the promotion rates were dropping along with it. Still, there was no limit to the disappointment of the knowledge that I wouldn t have a choice in the matter to stay or leave because that decision was going to be made for me. This was the same Army in which a few years prior we used to joke that as long as you had a pulse, you would make the promotion list to Major". This was devastating. I wondered how I would face the shame and explain what had happened to others. I had fallen so short of what was expected that I was having an extremely difficult time dealing with this. Though externally, it would look like it was business as usual for me, I was suffering greatly inside.

For the next several years, I continued to work arduously in my assigned positions and was fortunate to gain additional contacts and additional strong performance evaluations despite everything. However, throughout my final years in the Army, my anxiety was through the roof. It was an anxiety not only driven by continuing to work with a proverbial ax hanging over my head, but it was also driven from deep-seated shame, insecurities, and embarrassment. It was a significant gut check because, ultimately, I felt incredibly ashamed that I had let so many, including myself, down. I was a West Point graduate, a combat arms guy, Ranger tabbed, led a platoon in Iraq, and commanded a company of soldiers in Afghanistan. Yet, ultimately, though it mattered a lot to me, it did not amount to much in terms of success in my military career. What would others think of me? They must surely find it hard to see past my failures as well, right? I judged myself harshly because I felt it was deserved, and I started distancing myself from others.

Fortunately, I was able to find solace in other aspects of my life that would help to carry me through this dark time. One of the activities that helped me during this time was volunteering at a local charity to assist and mentor at-risk youth at an after school program that was part of a women s shelter. Not only did it provide me with perspective it provided me with an outlet where I felt I could still provide value to the community. Though my struggles were not anywhere close to what these children were dealing with, I could still empathize with where they were coming from since I was dealing with my own struggle. It was very impactful and I found a passion and love for mentoring others while doing it.

Initially, I was hesitant to reach out to others for help to figure out what my post-Army life would look like because I had false notions that I would be judged or that others would not provide me with their time. I couldn t have been more wrong about the reception that I would receive from everyone that I reached out to. Despite my initial hesitance to start reaching out, my classmates, fellow West Point graduates, and fellow veterans became an immense support source of support. They were all there for me and more. Without hesitation, every single person I reached out to was so generous with their most valuable resource – their time.

My fears of reaching out were completely unjustified. It's just amazing—the enduring connection that the military creates. I was picking up the phone and reconnecting with folks that I hadn't even talked to for around 10 years, and they were so willing to avail themselves. It was the same with veterans that I hadn t ever connected with prior to. I was looking for advice and information about different civilian careers and graduate school. I was not disappointed. Many, like me, had their own stories and had to overcome events where things had also gone less than perfectly. I learned that the network of veterans is vast and that there were numerous others who were more than willing to help a fellow vet in need. I came out much stronger and with a renewed perspective on life and my own worth that carried me through my transition out of the Army to where I am currently.

I ve taken my new perspective on life into my civilian career. I'm still here and I still have the ability to make a difference, help others, and be successful in my new career. Now, whenever there's an opportunity to help someone that I know is transitioning out of service into the civilian world, I'm the first person there. I want to pay it forward as I owe a lot to those that helped me through my transition. It s also the reason why I am in my current position as a commercial insurance broker with a focus on helping Veteran/Veteran-family run businesses. It s the ability to help that drove me to network with other Veterans who also focus on providing services to Veteran/Veteran-family run businesses.

Through one of these partnerships within the Veteran community, we ve developed a service that we launched in the second half of 2020, called Clarke and Sampson 4VETS. It provides commercial insurance solutions for veteran and veteran family-owned businesses. It s one way that I know that I can have a significant impact on the veteran community – by helping to protect their businesses. There s a lot of other great insurance brokers out there, but there are also a lot of less-than-stellar ones. I want to make sure that my brothers and sisters-in-arms get the best insurance advice possible from a source that they can trust to do right by them. I m fully aware that insurance brokers/agents don't necessarily have the best reputations, and I understand why, but there's a huge difference between someone that knows what they're doing and is committed to doing the right thing and what others might normally perceive to be an insurance agent.

I can t express how much the Veteran community was there for me when I needed it. When I was in the military, I did not understand the power of professional networking. The more people you know, the better you can help other people and be helped when you need it. Veteran-oriented networking groups fill in a gap to really empower military Vets through meaningful interactions. It's a really powerful thing, and I love connecting other Vets with these groups to help them see how much support is available within the community. It s all about Veterans helping out Veterans.

Never forget where you re coming from. Being a Veteran is definitely a unique and an increasingly uncommon denominator in our society. Those you serve with become like your family and, in many cases, closer than blood relatives. The bonds built while serving are extremely powerful, and very few people outside of the military will have that shared experience. This is even more evident now that I m a civilian. The shared experience of service to our country is, indeed, something special we share. Though my company is extremely supportive of the Veteran community, I'm the only veteran here. As a commercial insurance broker, I work with a lot of insurance carriers and their underwriters to obtain coverages for my clients. I ve only been able to work with one other underwriter that is a Veteran throughout my time in insurance. That s how rare we Veterans are in some industries. It makes it that much more important that Veterans do what they can to assist other Veterans when possible. The same people that would ve had your back in combat are the same people that often need your help in the civilian world.

Furthermore, I've often felt that a lot of the support for Veterans is superficial despite being well-intentioned. Most that haven t served will thank Veterans for their service in passing. but are not going to take it any further than that. Organizations often say they want to hire Vets, but don t take the time to really think about the value that veterans can provide their organizations. This is not necessarily the fault of anyone, it s just the nature of the military-civilian divide. However, this makes it more clear to me as to why Veterans should be able to find help from other Veterans who will provide them with the advice and mentorship that is needed to succeed in today s world.

To build a stronger, more supportive community, I strongly encourage Veterans to actively seek out other Vets. The potential impact of veterans helping out veterans is enormous. Oftentimes, it involves just a few phone calls or connecting someone with the right person. As I saw from my own transition into the civilian world, my brothers and sisters-in-arms were there for me. Whether it was connecting me with the right person or providing advice, I learned that I could count on them. The same goes for me. I ll always make myself available to the Veteran community. I ve been through some ups and downs and want to help other Veterans however I can. Whether it s providing advice from my experiences in the insurance business or taking on graduate school (Go Hoos!), it's very important to me to be able to share what I can. As I continue to grow personally and professionally, I look forward to providing even more substantial support in growing and supporting our Veteran community. I m working my way toward that goal, and I ll meet it along with the continued support from my brothers and sisters-in-arms.

Dan is a graduate of the United States Military Academy at West Point where he graduated with a degree in economics and commissioned as a second lieutenant in the US Army. Dan has served as an armor officer and a foreign area officer (FAO) throughout the world in various capacities to include multiple combat tours. While serving, Dan earned both his ranger tab and airborne wings. After leaving active duty service, Dan earned his Master of Science (MS) in Business Analytics from the University of Virginia's Darden School of Business and McIntire School of Commerce. Dan continues to live by the values "Duty, Honor, Country" ingrained in him through his experiences at West Point and service to the country.

Currently, Dan is a commercial insurance broker with Clarke & Sampson. One of the favorite parts of his job is assisting Veteran and Veteran Family-owned businesses with getting their insurance coverages right. Dan continues to give back to the Veteran Community by helping Veterans transitioning to civilian life, donating to Veteran charities via Clarke & Sampson 4VETs, and helping to facilitate networks where Veterans serve other Veterans.

Dan Yokoyama
Captain, USA
www.clarkeandsampson.com
https://www.linkedin.com/in/danyokoyama/

CHAPTER EIGHT

Lionel Hines

Networking is who I am

A lot of my initial veteran experiences go back to the Naval Academy. Because I started my service at the finest military institution on the planet, those experiences are considered "veteran experiences." It is safe to say, these experiences and networks would be similarly forged elsewhere, as most go back to friends I've made, football, and other mission-oriented experiences. The theme is just networking. I believe my veteran network just starts at a higher trust factor than most because of the affiliation to mission and service.

Networking is a large part of what I do as a person and a trait I've learned as a good follower and, subsequently, a leader. I went to the United States Naval Academy as a heavily recruited athlete in the Maryland-D.C. area. I was recruited by some premier NCAA Division I colleges, and the United States Naval Academy was one of those schools. This opportunity to attend a top-tier school and serve my country afterward was one of those opportunities that sparked my interest. The rigorous requirements for application and the extremely high bar for acceptance also made it a challenge worthy of my efforts. I knew two United States Naval Academy attendees, in my network, around my tenth-grade year. Each of those individuals was the epitome of academic excellence, and I considered it an honor to be mentioned in the same academic circle. My God-brother, LeRoy, had also relinquished a Pre-Med scholarship to Georgetown University to join the United States Army. That's how I got my introduction, if you will, to the military. In the eyes of this fifteen-year-old, you can imagine that the military was the cream of the crop.

In addition, my father, Roscoe, was a veteran. He was drafted into the Army during the Vietnam conflict. The extent of his military service was during the draft. He left the military after that, but he raised me with respect for service and country. My father was my idol. I say that with all sincerity. I idolized almost everything he did, and if the military helped him be successful, I counted this step as one of many more I should take.

I went to the Naval Academy Preparatory School, in Newport, Rhode Island. This school is an entryway for the Naval Academy, especially if you're going to redshirt in a sport or two. I didn't realize then, but that indoctrinating class of about 300 enlisted men and women forged bonds and relationships that would last forever. There's truth in the philosophy that people who struggle together, build a stronger bond together. There were skills, lessons, and experiences from the academy that would prepare me for life's trials—I just didn't realize it until later on. The one thing we learned right away was how to leverage the strengths of your teammates. Again, Networking.

As I met my company mates at the indoctrination period and then later my football teammates, I realized these would be the people who have earned the right to call me a brother and vice versa. Imagine a bootcamp setting, where no one knows the other, but you are placed into companies and demanded to cohabitate and accomplish missions. There we were, with these upper-class Naval Academy midshipmen, Coast Guard Academy cadets, and they're under the guidance of a Marine Corps drill sergeant. They've got a couple of different department head officers there, but their goal was to break us down. Break down a person from who they thought they were and then build us back up into the officer candidates they knew we could be.

I still have very close relationships with the people that I went through that struggle with. One of my closest friends, to this day, didn't meet the rigorous academic requirements to complete that school, but we've been durable friends and Life-Advisors for 30 plus years. A lot of that had to do with the fact that we went through that military indoctrination together. His room was one door over from me, during those first 60 to 90 days of indoctrination. He graduated from a completely different college, was a standout ROTC cadet and an exemplary Marine Corps officer. We've had a 30 plus year friendship on the back of that nine to ten months we shared, creating the foundation for trust and excellence.

I never really look at having "gotten out" of the military. It's funny that people will use that term and say, "Oh, when I got out." But I never really felt like I exited. I came out of the military to do private-sector work, but I've always felt tethered. I don't use that term all the time, but I still feel, very much, like I'm always a part of the military and how it's molded me into who I am today.

I can remember when I took my first private-sector job, and I was working for Nestle. I used a military officer headhunter as I went out to find a job. At my new company, the first thing they did was introduce me to the former military officers who shared similar backgrounds, colleges, and ambitions. Those were bonds of commonality that allowed me to learn quickly and prosper in that role. Three were former Army officers, and one was a Coast Guard officer. We immediately established a network of camaraderie, teamwork, and excellence. We celebrated each other's promotions and helped to navigate work miscues.

In addition to learning from those I worked with, I noticed I had an immediate bond and sense of respect for any service member that served in the Armed Forces. Twenty-five years ago, I purchased my first house. I had a neighbor, who retired from the Navy, a Machinist Mate first class. We immediately clicked socially and started telling these stories with our mutual chords of familiarity. We looked forward to sharing those stories. Even to this day, my neighbor-friend network is probably strongest in the veteran community. We treasure the opportunity to fellowship on Veteran's Day and engage in interservice banter. We remind each other to be proud of our service and thankful for the lives we share.

I would say that overall, I always sensed I would be allegiant to a veteran network if you will. That military sense of service and connectivity was always essential to me.

Navy Football Brotherhood

My allegiance to my football brotherhood, the guys I played football with while I was at the Naval Academy, that's another excellent illustration of leveraging co-laboring through trials with people. It was another level of building strong, almost unbreakable bonds. After you've been through all of the tests of indoctrination and academic rigor, in general, we forged even stronger bonds with the sport I love.

Many people think, if you go to a service academy and you're going to play football, it should be a distractor from the difficulties. This is not the case at all. Imagine, it's already challenging enough to get through a formidable institution like a military service academy. And if you're going to play an NCAA Division I sport, you're adding five hours into your day, studying film and physically training for a mentally and physically grueling sport. The objective (at least in football) is to try to dominate the opponent. Football is a Life-Sport. It reflects the challenges of continuously improving, sticking close to your teammates when things get tough, and getting up after you've been knocked down.

I always look back to my football brotherhood that shared military service as my extended family. The football network is so much bigger than me and my struggle. It is more about giving. This network comforts families and preserves the legacy of fallen brothers. The network teaches us how to mentor younger alumni and help nurture their goals and dreams. I'm indebted to this network just for the ability to participate.

The Transition

I felt like I was always received relatively well in the private-sector as a military service member. That also helped me find areas of commonality with other folks that were in the organization. I worked for multiple Fortune 500 companies, and at each of those, I've had a network where I can reach out to military veterans team members, where I could ask, "Hey, what do I need to do to succeed here?" or "What's is the next level of success?" Finding that network and building those bridges is everything when it comes to finding your place in the private-sector as you transition from the military.

As I think about my active-duty life, I had very clear-cut missions, and the mission didn't significantly change unless it was in a combat environment or there were quick dynamic changes from the top. We spend a lot of time training and preparing to do the mission, then by the time you're doing the mission, the mission is done precisely, as you've outlined it. In contrast, the private-sector missions are so much more ambiguous. There are so many different opportunities. Also, the priorities change significantly in short periods of time. I found strategic planning has always been something I leveraged from my military service experience. Strategic planning helps align everyone to the most significant mission and then cascades that mission to lower-level objectives. The team decentralizes to achieve the overall strategy but doesn't sway with conflicting opportunities. I often leverage strategic planning military experiences to remain flexible and have contingencies in place for the private-sector.

However, there are times when I realized private sector missions are significantly different from strategic military missions. They can be frustrating because they change, in the private sector, so much more rapidly than in the military. One example: In the military, every year, a particular training is going to be in Hawaii, or the training is going to be held in Fort Polk, Louisiana, or it's going to be in this specific location. In the private-sector, we would have a key conference that I have to attend next week in Paris, and, suddenly, the priority will change that, and an organization leader will say, "You know what? I need you in New Orleans, instead, to attend this peripheral vascular conference because I've got too many physicians scheduled to attend New Orleans."

I think those are stark differences between military training and the private- sector. Also, in the private sector, at least in Sales, every day is combat. My training had to take place daily before I ever left my house. The terrain changed so frequently that it was imperative to study the new data, listen to your competitor's approach, and practice objection handling. In the military, we trained for months, maybe years, on one or two approaches.

Veteran Networks

There are multiple veteran networks of which I am a part, each on a different level of connectivity. Here, I will share a few: The National Naval Officers Association, The National Negro Association of Naval Officers, The Black Service Academy Network, The Service Academy Business Masterminds Network, Naval Academy Alumni Association, and White Feather Investments. Some of the networks are business-related. Many of the networks are for finding like-minded individuals and social outlets. On most occasions, the network is a means of association and representation. I use these networks as a way for me to make a statement about myself to others, so others can identify who I am by organizational association.

I think about the Navy Football Brotherhood, how we established and incorporated it. We were all going back to football games and tailgating the Army-Navy games. Those tailgates require a high degree of planning. One of the brothers was assigned to the team as an athletic program officer. He considered the mentorship aspect for the current players as they reached the fleet. He hosted a meeting before a big tailgate, and that was the catalyst. We initially incorporated it to ensure we had a place for the brothers to reconnect and fellowship together when attending football games. I felt like that was worth investing in and repeating, and we had a lot of great guys that put together the time and the energy to incorporate. At the time of incorporation, that network started at under a hundred former players. Now it's into the thousands of former Navy Football players in the network. That is an excellent example of the strength of brotherhood and those unbreakable bonds. That veteran network is connected back through the Naval Academy Alumni Association. It's connected back through the Naval Officers Association, which is linked through several other networks. I encourage veterans, especially veteran entrepreneurs to explore other avenues that will continue to grow relationships, within the veteran community.

Diverse Experiences and Credibility

At the time of this book, I'm currently a Vice President of Channel Alliances (Sales). My life experiences are diverse, and I've never felt locked into any specific career path. I've led almost hundreds for less than $35k/year, and I've managed only myself and been compensated well over a half-million $500k/year. My career path has varied, and I've always approached life with a "what's next?" attitude. My hope for this book is to help someone realize they can achieve any goal they desire, and their veteran experience can be an advantage.

My example of diverse experiences is remarkable in many regards. As my colleagues have mentioned, I've been a leader on one of the most elite military special warfare units ever assembled. On the one hand, I've supported missions for U.S. Special Operations Command, to protect the homeland and U.S. interests abroad. On the other hand, I've helped promote the use of life-saving medical device technologies, in healthcare facilities worldwide. I've greeted custodial staff by their first name on my way to have lunch with the organization's CEO. My goal in life is to treat people with respect and help connect others to their purpose. Purpose is confused with a job but, in my humble opinion, purpose is what you were born to do.

I remember starting off in the private-sector, doing production supervision, logistical planning, and supply chain. I got a taste of commercial sales by leading a Customer Service department and then transitioned to National Account Sales and, later, direct sales. I've been a leader in multiple Fortune 500 companies, and my leadership experience spans over thirty years. I can say with confidence, success all boils back down to the ability to network and then building upon those networks.

Networks can change your life

When I was twelve, I would complete odd jobs for money. I had a host of regular clients that I would service; cutting grass, shoveling snow, painting, etc. By the time I was in High School, I could earn more money than my friends, who worked traditional part-time hours. Two of the most valuable lessons I learned, were owning my entrepreneurial success and building a network of love. As a result of those formative years, I have the most endearing and sincerely loving relationships with one of my "then clients" and "now family."

Our relationship has grown to an unconditional display of love, rivaled only by parental love. I'm so grateful for the opportunity we share to participate in each other's lives. That wonderful couple often reflects on how they witnessed my early signs of leadership. They recount how I often incentivized my friends to help me accomplish those odd jobs while fellowshipping and rewarding them with something they desired. One day, they noticed I had a whole team with me as I finished their landscaping.

They called it leadership. I call it networking. Imagine, my football team needed bonding time, so we would swim at my parent's home and go to the buffet for lunch. We stayed in shape, stayed out of trouble, and the money made paid for everyone's lunch. To this day, those networks of love are still intact. The foundation of that High School team went on to compete for a championship. The Fountains are still pouring love, advice, and guidance into my teenage children and me.

Networking Helps Us Lead

When I first started working in medical devices, I was leading Manufacturing but was soon asked to lead Manufacturing, Engineering, and Design. Although an Engineer by schooling, I didn't have medical device experiences in my background. I was highly familiar with leading; however, medical device manufacturing wasn't anything I had experience leading. I leveraged a newfound veteran network to understand the organization's needs and how my strengths would align. One of my managers was a former Marine Corps Sergeant. Three of my co-workers were former naval officers. Two were Naval Academy alumni, and I built a successful career in that organization, partnering with a life-long veteran friend. I met her networking at that job. As a result, I currently hold patents in medical device technology. I developed intellectual property and made significant process improvements that have changed how medical device companies can manufacture.

The powerful networks are still intact. My close partner retired as an Admiral in the US Navy Reserves and was appointed by the President as the Director of the Small Business Administration. We leverage our veteran friendship and network to accomplish life and work missions because we trust one another. We have a foundation of trust built on service to our country.

Find a Need and Fill It

As I continued to network and followed the "needs," I moved toward the commercial-sales environment. In 2008, I was leading a Customer Service, Distribution, and Logistics Operations department. My company had just finished the largest acquisition in medical device history. As a result of the negotiations, we ended up co-licensing our flagship product with our biggest competitor. We were both trying to sell the same product in the marketplace, so we immediately commoditized that product overnight. As a result of the commoditization, both companies needed different relationships in Sales. The physician was no longer the only decision-maker. Physician preferences were quickly fading in medical device procurement and what you are now more familiar with are larger buying group organizations that buy for healthcare, grew in influence. Before this commoditization, organizations would have stayed in an area, where product quality was not distinguishable. Like, gloves, gowns, wipes, etc.. Group Purchasing didn't get their power until they started leveraging their pricing across the industry. At the time, my company needed people that had relationships with Buying Groups, and they needed them in a hurry.

As a Customer Service leader, I developed a solid network with hospital administrators. These Administrators were the buying professionals with power over the purchase but dared not encroach on physician preference items. Many of my administrator relationships leveraged my veteran background. Ultimately, I took the tools that I was using in Supply Chain. The tools I used to hold my vendors accountable in routine meetings. I stated, "These are the metrics I wanted to see when my suppliers visited me for meetings," and "These are the relationships we need to build as their suppliers." I turned those around and used them to network with large buying group organizations, much more built like supply chain managers. This strategy opposed the direct physician preference sell, which focused on the cardiovascular interventionalist, surgeon or the peripheral vascular interventionalist/surgeon. That's the old model of med device sales. I was transformational in our organization's adoption of this new strategy. It became imperative when we commoditized our flagship product overnight. When our largest competitor had the same product that forced these leading MedDev companies to change our selling models.

I was fortunate because a lot of that strategic change resulted in me being in the right place, at the right time, to build the right network. Once I transitioned into sales fully, it became essentia to leverage relationships from the military and fellow veterans who were selling med devices. Some of those allies included physicians and surgeons, who were more than willing to partner with me. Of that network, a close friend and co-author, Captain Suzanne Lesko. Suzanne worked in Sales, Marketing and Consulting in her civilian capacity, and our introduction began as fellow service members in Point Loma, CA.
[December 2, 2011- Suzanne Lesko and Lionel Hines, Point Loma, CA]

[Dec 2nd, 2011- Suzanne Lesko and Lionel Hines, Point Loma, CA]

Suzanne and I would serve together in a different capacity years later. While deployed to the Horn of Africa, Suzanne was the Public Affairs Officer (PAO) to the Special Operations. She was well versed in our training and missions. In fact, she was responsible for the daily briefings which went directly to the highest levels of our government. As a result of our prior service together in multiple capacities and network connectivity, we shared a special bond, and still do to this day.

Similarly, many of these service-connected prioritized missions helped to build a bond between Mark Mhley and me. We also served together with Joint Special Operations Command (JSOC) where we worked to execute many multi-faceted operations. We must have met daily over video teleconference (VTC). I was forward deployed and he was in Virginia Beach. Only after working with each other for months, did we have a chance to meet in Virginia and learn about our common Naval Academy background.

Never Coincidence

Years later, I was linking up with another veteran network referred to me by a newly contracted sales agent. She was incredibly bright and outgoing. I was glad to add her to my Sales team. She was also married to a West Point graduate actively involved in Service Academy Business Masterminds (SABM). It was probably seven years after Mark and I served together at Joint Special Operations Command, and I'm speaking with the CEO of the Service Academy Business Masterminds. He says, "Hey, you should probably know, I've got a guy who's also doing something in payment processing. You two should talk." He gives me Mark's name and information. In this fashion, I reached out to Mark, but I didn't recognize the name, because Mark and I didn't use our actual names when serving together with JSOC. It wasn't until we got on a virtual call that we recognized each other from seven years ago. It was funny, that connection inspired us to work together. We knew, whatever we needed to do to make things work for us, we would do it. Now we leverage our business models to further the network of veterans and veteran spouses. PaymentLOCK4Vets was born to help veteran entrepreneurs.

That's just a few examples of networks and how powerful they can be in your life. "...I know this guy. he's also a Naval Academy graduate. You're working in the same field, and maybe you guys should talk." That was a throw over the bridge from a service connection and resulted in the reconnection of a brother from over seven years prior. I will tell you that my first comment to my partner was, "Oh, this is a brother of mine. I don't care what we have to do to make this business work for each other. We'll figure it out because we served in a place where my team relied on his team, and lives were at stake. We operated 'No Fail' missions. For those that aren't familiar, "No Fail Missions" are missions that don't have a failure option.

Honor - Courage - Commitment

The military brotherhood is without a doubt, one of the most important connections that I have. It defines who I am to a large degree, my sense of service and pride. don't just mean from my network. I mean my sense of service and my sense of pride. I think about my service to this country, how much I love my country and the next level of commitment. Honor, Courage and Commitment.

If we can go back to what I mentioned earlier, what have I done? When you've served with someone, and you've been through a trial, you've earned the right to call them a brother or a sister. That's the same way I feel about my veteran network. We get to that point where if you've worn the uniform and you've signed a blank check, where the value is up to and including your life, that's pretty important, and a bond that is not easily shaken.

Veteran Advice:

- Build and create a network from every experience
- Love, cherish, and support that network into your passions
- Leverage your network and success to benefit both

Lionel Hines
Lieutenant Commander, USN
LGHines@me.com\
https://paymentlock.com/
https://www.linkedin.com/company/paymentlock/

CHAPTER NINE

Robyn Grable

My story is not your immediate image of combat or conflict. I did not serve in combat. But I raised my right hand to defend our country and every day for nearly nine years, I trained for the unexpected, safeguarded our freedom through my work and proudly put on the uniform. What I experienced however, within the military was certainly conflict. It was 1979 and I joined the Navy just after graduating high school in a small town in Indiana. I did not have money for college, but school was where I shined and felt like somebody. At the time, I was looking for direction. I wanted to be a part of something, and I needed someone to stand up for me. I came from a split family—I had two sets of parents. Both my biological father and my stepfather were alcoholics. My mother was co-dependent and my stepmother abusive. I felt alone and lost through much of my life. I had an imaginary friend when I was six. I learned later in life that inventing imaginary friends is a coping mechanism and some say, visible guardian angels.

My dream was to be a child psychologist because in my mind, I could somehow protect children by being in that profession. Someone to stand up for the children. Someone to advocate for them, be their voice and protect them. Without prospects for college, I decided on the Navy simply because the recruiter came to my high school and told us, Join the Navy and see the world!" While I was exploring it more, it didn t take very long for me to know, it was the right decision for me. I was so excited to join and see parts of the world outside of Indiana.

I had never been on an airplane before. My ears became clogged from the altitude and my first night at basic training was pure torture. Going through basic training, however, was incredible. I loved it. I excelled at it. I ended up becoming one of five new recruits who were chosen to become assistant company commanders right after I graduated basic training. In 1979 they did not have enough female company commanders which is what they called drill instructors in the Navy. I immediately transitioned from being the trainee to the trainer. It was pretty awesome, and something I am extremely proud of. It became clear, very quickly, in this first assignment with the Navy, that I could help someone who was struggling.

I have always been someone who fights for the underdog because, as a stepchild, I was the underdog of my family. While my fighting spirit did not start in the Navy, the Navy gave me solid footing to stand up for myself and others. Early on I experienced two types of men in the Navy. There were the grandfather types who would put their arms around you to try and protect you or they would simply tell you could not do this or that because you were a woman. Then there were the men who believed the only reason women were in the military was because they were promiscuous. I did not want anything to do with either of those archaic stereotypes. I wanted to stand on my own and being told you can t" only fueled me to fight harder.

The first time I went off base in my uniform however and walked out into the crowd of civilians after we graduated was exhilarating for me. Being able to wear that uniform and know that not everybody can do it, not everybody will do it, made me very, very proud. I loved, loved, loved being in the Navy. I was honored to wear the uniform, and extremely critical of those who didn't wear it properly.

After basic training in Orlando, I left for Iceland in 1980. I remember saying to the Yeoman (HR) when he gave me the assignment, where in the world is Iceland?" After a nine-hour flight on a C-130, I arrived in a foreign country, to a place that experienced six months of nearly 24 hours of darkness and six months of nearly 24 hours of light. Iceland is a beautiful country, truly spectacular with its glaciers and hidden hot spring pools. One of my greatest learning experiences happened in the office of Captain Robert Berg. The Commander of Naval Air Station Keflavik at the time. One morning while I was cleaning his office, Captain Berg arrived early. I was terrified as an E-2 being in the presence of the boss".

He showed me the utmost kindness and told me, Officers deserve respect for the positions they have earned, but we are just human beings and we put on our uniform the same as you, one leg at a time. Give respect but never be afraid." His words inspired me in many ways that I have carried with me to this day.

I did not have a designation or occupation yet (which is why I was on cleaning duty), so I had to pick my role—my military job. I was told I could not work in a submarine because I was a woman. I was told I could not work on a radar plane because I was a woman. I was told I could not do this or that solely because I was a female. I had to pick a female" role and I reluctantly accepted a job in data processing. Even with the strife of choosing, it turned out to be a rocking career choice! During my time in the Navy, I programmed charts before there was Excel. I mined data and wrote reports on the whereabouts of Russian submarines. It was information that was vital to our national security. I processed payroll on keypunch cards and operated the largest computer system in the country at the time. Even though I found a career I loved, there were still struggles. Remember this is 1980. There was no internet. There were no cell phones or FaceTime. We had land lines but could only call long distance from Command Operations and we could only do that once a month or every other month. I was a naïve, country girl exposed to some very scary things.

The atmosphere and environment of an isolated duty station where temperatures didn t rise above 40 degrees in the summer, presented its own challenges. There was not a lot to do in Iceland outside of work, nearly everything centered on partying indoors. The men on deployment were away from their wives or girlfriends and when they weren t out on a mission, everyone was at the bar or some sort of party. Insecure and misjudged females, men on a hall pass, and alcohol. Not a good combination.

No question, I loved, loved, loved being in the Navy. My life in the Navy was not without professional accomplishments and great memories. I was honored for the work that I did. I received a Navy achievement medal, Navy commendations and rapid advancement. Within eight years, I had advanced from E-2 to E-7. Through the years though, I got tired of hearing, "It's the way the Navy's always done it, and it s the way they'll always do it." I believed if I became an officer, I could change the Navy. Talk about an underdog fight! Being enlisted, the Navy offered two options to become an officer. Warrant Officer and Limited Duty Officer. It is not an easy process. It must be earned. I worked really, really hard to complete the requirements and present the highest standard of character, leadership and capabilities to be considered for the limited duty officer program. According to my Commanding Officer, whose signature/approval I needed for submission, my package was stellar. Sadly, the Navy decided not to rate any data processing limited duty officers that year. The selection committee did not even open the package, and no one ever looked at it.

When I found that out, I was devastated and disenchanted. My heart was broken because I truly thought I could affect change and do more for the Navy as an officer. At the same time, I had just made E-7, Chief Petty Officer, and was very proud of my accomplishment. However, the Navy had a very, very punishing and humiliating initiation ritual they put people through when you make E-7. Although I understand that it is a rite of passage, it was terrifying having just watched my husband go through it. I wanted no part of it. Of course, if you didn't go through it, you ultimately wore the uniform, but you weren't seen" as a true chief petty officer. Compounding the stress, after three years in Hawaii and only seeing my family once, I was facing orders to California as a single parent. Even though it was stateside, it was across the country where I, once again, would not have any family support. Considering these factors played heavily into my decision to get out of the military three months shy of nine years.

Another dark and confusing time happened during my tour in Jacksonville, FL. A supervisor lured me into a situation that I never saw coming. Six months pregnant, out to dinner with the team for my farewell, he assaulted me. When I was able to get away, he threatened to cancel my orders to Maine where my husband was stationed, if I told anyone what had happened. Young and with just under four years in the Navy, I fell prey to those who wielded their power and unacceptable behavior on others. Although I told my roommate what happened, I didn t report him because I was afraid. Afraid I d have to stay in that horrible place, reliving that moment over and over. I think I was also in shock. Did that really just happen? For all those out there who are brave enough to report these incidents, thank you.

The fall of 1985, marked five moves in six years. I had been transferred from Orlando, to Iceland to Jacksonville, FL to Brunswick, ME and found myself stationed in Pearl Harbor. It s Hawaii and most definitely paradise. The historical reverence is everywhere and can t be missed. Although I was living in paradise it was also far, far away from loved ones. No cell phones, no internet, and a six-hour time difference. That kind of isolation can take its toll. But it was there that I formed yet another advocacy group for women in the military, as I had done at each duty station before. It was a safe harbor. A place to go and feel protected. It was another example of my time in the military being a time of working for the other veterans, for their successes, their troubles, and their challenges. To this day, I vividly remember a woman service member who approached me. She was struggling with among other things, alcoholism. She reached out for help, attended our advocacy group, and told me she felt she could trust me. I could relate to her on many levels and knew that I needed the women of the advocacy group as much as they needed me. That was 30 years ago, and it still gives me goosebumps and brings me to tears.

One of the brightest spots during my time in the Navy is the birth of my daughter. She was born while I was stationed in Brunswick/Topsham, Maine in October 1983. She is my proudest moment and remains my proudest to this day. While I was only allowed 30 days leave after she was born, it was only a couple of years prior to her birth, that females were discharged when they became pregnant while serving. Still, the tides of equality were uneven as I faced having to give up custody of her if I wanted to serve on a Navy ship. Even though the only ships women were able to serve aboard were not combat related, they were not allowed to have dependents *and* serve on ships. These experiences, I believe, only helped to make me a better advocate for all.

Although she doesn t have memories of it, except from pictures and stories I tell her, my daughter lived in three different states before her fifth birthday. Had we taken the orders to California, it would have been four. The two of us traveled from Maine to Hawaii alone while her father went through SERE school in California before he could join us. With my fourteen month old daughter in tow, I made the trip and got ourselves settled in a time zone six hours away. Returning from Hawaii with orders to complete programming school in Quantico, VA, my daughter and I drove from California to Virginia, alone. The resourcefulness and resilience of military spouses or dependents should never be questioned.

I chose to leave the Navy in 1988. I completely put it behind me and did not reconnect with the military until many years later. While working on my master's in psychology, I met an Army veteran's wife who had told me her husband had been out for about six months and could not get an interview—he could not find a job. He was feeling depressed and worthless. Something took over that day and made me remember what I went through when I transitioned out of the Navy.

Never having a resume, I went to a resume writer and he told me my best option was to be an administrative assistant. No one will understand what you did in the military. We don't know how to translate your skills. You're a female, no one's going to understand why you were in the military in the first place, so you don't want that to be held against you." At the time I didn't realize what was to come, but I instantly became underemployed, underpaid, and undervalued. I became another statistic. Every year, over 200,000 service members transition back to civilian life. They have faced down our enemies, spread goodwill in under-developed countries, provided disaster relief, search and rescue/recovery and protected our resources, our country and our freedom. As veterans, we demonstrate the courage, resilience, and adaptability that are hallmarks of the American military. Our businesses and communities need that leadership, experience, and character, but the gap between military service and civilian employment continues to widen.

I did have a positive experience when I moved to California (yes, I should have stayed in the Navy if I was moving to California anyway). I went for a job interview, and met the hiring manager, he was from Japan. He barely said anything to me during the interview, but when I got the job, the American manager came in and said, "When he saw that you were a Navy veteran, he immediately said, Hire her.'" A great example of the two schools of thought—people who didn't care to understand military experience and people that recognized right away the value in it.

It was not until recently that it clicked for me. I recognized that there had to be a better way. It wasn t right, not only for females, but for all military personnel who were transitioning out as well as their spouses too. This began my fight for the value a person brings, not just whether they are male or female, what ethnicity they are, or any other orientation they may have. The support groups and safe harbors I was a part of creating would lead me to who I am today in civilian life. As an advocate for our veterans and military families, I stand up for their skills as they transition into civilian life, breaking barriers and misperceptions, and helping them find great careers with a new purpose.

Current job boards, job fairs or even direct hire placement services do not fill the gap on connecting employers and the highly skilled candidates within the military talent pool. I created Veterans ASCEND for all of these reasons. To fight for the recognition of skills, to end underemployment for veterans and military spouses, and to ensure those who have served our country continue to belong to something great and feel valued for what they bring to the table—not to be misunderstood, set aside or underemployed.

While the Navy became part of the fiber of my being, it was not until I left the Navy, sadly, that I realized how connected I was—on a family level—with my brothers and sisters in service. I took it for granted and I am very happy to have it back today. So, in addition to my work, what keeps me connected to the military now, is my grandchildren. Telling them stories, showing them about the military, and making them proud of people who serve. I am honored to pass down this history, especially to a generation who has seen less and less of the population serve in uniform.

Today, my career purpose is back. I work with veterans every day. Not just from the Navy, but every branch, and every era. Obviously, being a Navy veteran, anytime I meet another Navy veteran, I'm asking when they served, could we have crossed paths many years ago, were they stationed in the same place I was stationed? I instantly feel a connection to somebody that served at the same duty stations that I did. Even if they weren't there the same years that I was, we were there together, we were in that place together. Every service member, veteran, or military spouse I meet, there's always a connection, no matter how small.

Closer to home, my nephew is an active-duty Marine and after two years we were finally able to meet for dinner. I got to hug him for the first time since he was stationed on the west coast and deployed to the Middle East twice. Proudly, he recently made sergeant E-5, he just re-enlisted and he plans to do his twenty or more. We discussed his housing allowance and all the things the military provides. When service members transition out, it can be a huge eye opener on the cultural and financial differences. What we are doing at Veterans ASCEND, is helping to bridge that transition from leaving a most intrinsic culture to a community where there are no rule books on when you sleep, what you eat, or where you can go.

Extensive military roots run through me and connectivity with all branches is deep within me. I've mentored veterans through Veterans Treatment Court, have family members who served in the Air Force, and my favorite uncle, a Vietnam War veteran, was severely wounded while serving in the Army. It's easy to look back and say that I should ve made a different decision to stay in the Navy longer, but I also believe that everything happens for a reason. I was meant to do what I did for the time I was in, get out, have the transition experience, and then find the path to today. And I absolutely love what I do, even without a uniform on, I get to be connected to the military every day.

For those in transition, it is all about the connections. At Veterans ASCEND, we make employment connections electronically for the veterans and military spouses by translating their occupations and experience into a skills profile. Our algorithm automatically matches the candidates to employers. We also stay connected through social media, webinars and other events. We utilize and partner with the people we know to help others be known".

The reality is that in today's market, no matter what you want to do it's about connections, it's about who knows you and who they can connect you to. It's not about applying for jobs online, going into something blindly or hoping to attend a job fair and find the career you want. For military talent, applying online is successful about 5% of the time. Rather than spending time writing and rewriting a resume (ask 1,000 people and you will get 1,000 different answers on how to format a resume), spend time making meaningful connections. It's also important for people in transition to start early. You have to do the work to make connections, building your network of fellow veterans and civilians. Think of it as an investment. If you put money in the bank when you're in your 20s, by the time you re 40, your bank account will be significantly larger. Start collecting those resources, networks, and connections now, and it will pay off exponentially in the future.

An important note, it s not always about what they can do for you, but what you can also do for others. It s important to make sure you are offering to help your connections in some way. Keep our military family strong and make sure they know, "Hey, if you need something from me, just reach out, because I want to give back as much as I get from my network."

Veterans ASCEND is about making employment connections automatically for our service members, veterans, and military family. Veterans ASCEND is an AI-powered Talent Sourcing platform. It s an intentional model to transform how companies connect with talent and build inclusivity into their organization. Our proprietary technology translates occupations into a skills profile. Not just a titles translator. We dive deeper to create a consequential list of skills that align to the direct skills needed in the civilian workforce. We looked at every job description and training materials to translate the role into a skills profile. No other program does this automatically. Other programs match titles but not the actual skills. They pigeonhole a veteran and perpetuate the misperception that occupations like infantry can only do security or data processing technicians can only do computer programming. We recognize the skills a stay-at-home military spouse brings to the workforce. Resilience, resourcefulness, flexibility, adaptability – all define what it takes to find out you are moving in fifteen days and you have to have your family ready. These are skills every employer needs and misses out on by making assumptions and pre-judgments about military talent.

Unlike other programs, we match veterans and military families directly with employers who are intentionally hiring and valuing military talent for their skills and experience. We do not pull jobs from the internet or an employer s job board. Our subscribers must create job profiles and pick the exact skills they need for each one. They can create an unlimited number of job profiles and our candidates can match to more than one. This allows the employer to see how a veteran or military spouse fits across their organization. It is a fundamental paradigm shift in the foundational old way of applying with or reviewing a resume. It is about aligning the candidate based on skills. No more translating resumes, guessing about qualifications, sitting through job fairs or missing out on hiring the right military talent for the employer.

Veterans ASCEND jump starts, compliments, and accelerates an employer s military hiring initiatives. We provide employers the flexibility and mobility to create a pipeline of qualified candidates always at the ready. Decreasing time to fill. Increasing productivity and retention. Utilizing Veterans ASCEND saves time and money in sourcing great talent. Employers can then spend more time on interviewing, onboarding and retaining top talent. HR and Talent Acquisition turn from being viewed as an expense item to the important cog that increases revenue through improved productivity and reduced turnover.

Our service is free for all military members and families. No resume. No search. No applying first. There is a well-known saying Never judge a book by its cover." With less than 1% of Americans serving in uniform, military talent needs an approach that allows them to put their best foot forward by showcasing their skills and aptitudes. Rather than being filtered out and overlooked because a person doesn t understand their resume. Employment is essential to a successful transition. When veterans comprise nearly a quarter of all U.S. suicide deaths, not having a civilian career that values their talents, challenges them and pays them their worth, could be the catalyst that starts the spiral of abuse and struggle to find reasons to stay alive. Serving in the military, a higher purpose is drilled into us from day one. Regardless of the era, every service member knows that lives are on the line when they do their job. And their job is 24/7. My passion and new purpose is doing whatever we can to help someone, especially in finding employment after service. Veterans ASCEND creates transformational possibilities, opening doors and moving employers past the stereotypes, myths and simple lack of knowledge.

I couldn t be on this journey without my wonderful family. Their support and love give me the strength to carry my gratitude forward. I am immensely honored and proud to be part of our military community and share my individual story in this anthology of patriotism, courage, and advocacy for all, no matter what gender, ethnicity, life choices, or mistakes. In this book you will read insightful chapters from fellow veterans. We are all a family, we are all connected, and we will be forever.

Robyn Grable is the Founder and CEO of Veterans ASCEND, which she created to connect employers and military talent, improving corporate bottom lines as well as the lives of America s service heroes and their families. Her unwavering commitment to veteran employment is well-served by her corporate and military experience, including more than 30 years of private sector human resources after nine years of service in the U.S. Navy. Her ongoing study of America s veteran workforce have made her a leading voice on the barriers and keys to success for their employment. In the private sector she focused primarily on workforce management, human capital planning, recruitment, process and procedure evaluation, strategic alignment and relationship management. She created skills assessment programs at blue chip companies **McDonald s Corporation** and **McGraw-Hill** and during her tenure as a **Strategic Client Partner at ADP**, a leading human capital management firm, Robyn successfully managed and grew the largest client portfolio of Fortune 100 companies. **Today she is focused entirely on ensuring veterans and military spouses are recognized for their skills, valued for their talent and that America s employers realize the full value and skills of America s heroes and military spouses, poised in the civilian workforce to truly ascend.**

Robyn Grable
First Class Petty Officer, USN
https://linkedin.com/in/robyn_grable
robyn@veteransascend.com
https://veteransascend.com

CHAPTER TEN

Scott Chesson

As the son of a retired Air Force MSGT who served in Vietnam from 1968-1969, I have always been positively influenced by veterans. My mother is also an Air Force veteran. In fact, my parents met while they were both serving in the military. My dad retired when I was 11 years old in 1973. Additionally, my older brother served in the Navy for four years.

You could say that being in the military was in my DNA. The military has always and will always be a part of my life. I freely admit that I often get choked up when the national anthem plays before a sporting event. I like to sing along to the national anthem although my voice leaves a lot to be desired. Being a vet myself, that's just the way I think and the way I do things. I try to do everything with honor and integrity and represent the United States Naval Academy and the United States Military with dignity. It s how I approach everything that I do. It s this desire to uphold the integrity and respect that drives my passion about veteran s issues.

I was rather young when the Vietnam War was going on. It ended in '75. I served mostly in the 80s, and it was a completely different time for the military than the 60s and the 70s. The 80s were kind of like a resurgence of the military, the way it was treated by the public. It was a big buildup to try to put the Soviet Union out of business. I served with a lot of people who served in Vietnam. It was very interesting to get their perspective. It was a completely different era of public perception of the military. I did not fully realize the implications of my dad going to Vietnam when it happened. It only occurred to me much later that he may not have come back.

I recall the poor reception for returning Vietnam veterans in the 1970s and the dichotomy of my sister and others wearing MIA or POW bracelets to commemorate those missing or captured in Vietnam. My collective memories and experiences starting with my dad have always engendered a special place in my heart for all veterans. Especially Vietnam vets.

While my dad was in Vietnam, we had a map on the wall that showed Vietnam and the surrounding countries. The only city I can recall from the map is Phnom Penh, which is in Cambodia. He sent me and my two brothers each a hat at Christmas that resembled the hat from the picture below:

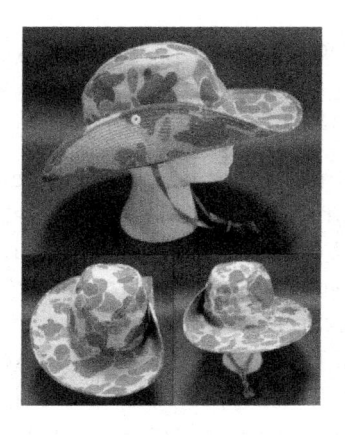

My mom was from a family of six kids in Ohio and needed a real adventure, so she enlisted. That's how she and my dad met. My dad was at the University of North Carolina and he wanted to be an Air Force pilot, as probably a lot of people wanted to be in the early 50s. He found out he was color blind, and I think he was really devastated so he never finished college, and instead he dropped out and enlisted in the Air Force. He was in Air Force reconnaissance and photo interpretation. I was very lucky to have such terrific parents. Just great, great role models and they really have always affected me very positively. I know that everybody is not that fortunate, but I have been incredibly lucky to have that background.

You learn a lot in a military family environment. The lesson I learned quickly was that there was a special bond, and they are all a great group of people by and large. They're from all over the country and all over the world, and it's a bond that doesn't go away. To this day I go out of my way to help vets. I have a tremendous affinity for them.

My own military career was quite different. I applied for admission to both the Naval and Air Force Academies. I received a Presidential nomination to the Naval Academy (for sons and daughters of career military veterans). I then received an appointment to Annapolis. I received a nomination to the Air Force Academy and an appointment to the Air Force s preparatory school in Minnesota. I decided to go to Annapolis for a variety of reasons including the uncertain prospects of spending a year in cold Minnesota before heading to Colorado Springs. I grew up all over the place but mostly in warm climates (Panama, Georgia, North Carolina, and Hawaii).

My military career spanned from my induction at Annapolis in July 1980 until my assignment to the IRR (individual ready reserve) in the fall of 1991.

I was not a model midshipman or a flawless officer. However, I would not trade any of the memories, leadership lessons, mistakes made, and experiences for an easier path. I learned from my mistakes and consider the U.S. military to be the greatest leadership laboratory in the world. There is an inherent truth to learning the greatest amount from your mistakes.

One of the things my dad would always tell me, I was an E-7, The one thing you have to remember is you're going to be an officer and you want to make sure that you really respect and value your men and women because they know a heck of a lot more than you do and should not be underestimated. . I took that advice to heart in my career in the military and beyond. It was spot on.

I was stationed on FF 1048, the USS SAMPLE (a Garcia class frigate), in Pearl Harbor from 1985-1987 (picture at the conclusion of this chapter is of me with the SAMPLE behind me in Vancouver, BC in 1986). My last division officer billet on the Sample was the First Lieutenant. The First Lieutenant leads the deck and seamanship division manned by boatswain s mates. I greatly enjoyed working with this group of straightforward, salt of the earth sailors. I spent a considerable amount of time at Captain s Mast with the BMs advocating for them when they got in trouble. Fortunately, I was intimately familiar with Captain s Mast from my previous division officer job as Main Propulsion Assistant (MPA). The machinist mates (MMs) and boiler technicians (BTs) were also salt of the earth sailors and seemed to find trouble as much as the boatswain s mates.

When I was the First Lieutenant, I worked with a Senior Chief (E-8) who had served on a PBR in Vietnam. One of my fondest memories as an officer and a veteran was when the Senior Chief took me and our two first class Boatswain s mates to the Chiefs club at the end of my tour. It is indeed a rare honor for a division officer to receive an invite to the Chiefs club.

At the end of my tour on the Sample in September 1987, I took a MAC flight to Australia. During the flight, I encountered some Vietnam veterans heading to Australia to participate in a Vietnam Veteran s welcome home parade in Sydney. I enjoyed speaking to them and told them how my dad served and how I greatly respected their service. I thought their reception after serving in Vietnam was a raw deal. They were appreciative and gave me a medal (pictured below). I was very touched. I came across this medal recently while my wife and I were doing some file clean-up.

I left active duty in May 1990 and stayed in the reserves until the fall of 1991. The aspect I missed the most after leaving active duty and the reserves was the camaraderie of interacting regularly with veterans having a common background. The highlight by far of the reserves was the camaraderie.

It was a hole that I filled occasionally for the next twenty years by attending Navy football games with my classmates from Annapolis, the occasional class reunion, and alumni meetings. However, I never lost the veteran connection and I have always felt a special affinity for people I have encountered who are veterans.

After attending graduate school at UNC-Chapel Hill in 1991, I started my business career with IBM. My ultimate goals in business were to become a chief financial officer or run my own business. I worked for 8 companies in 29 years in business. I always had a certain restlessness that I sometimes attribute to my background as both a son of a career military veteran and a veteran myself.

I was a CFO/COO of the last five companies I worked for from 1999-2020. The companies were smaller with less than 150 employees. I discovered that I enjoyed working for smaller businesses so that I could have a greater impact. Like my experience of being on a smaller ship with a complement of 250 sailors. I employed many of the leadership lessons gleaned from my experience as a naval officer. I detected a shortage at times of ethics and accountability during my business career.

During my business career, I was approached several times over the years by veterans or service academy grads desiring mentoring or advice on how to make the transition into a business career. I thoroughly enjoyed the opportunity to connect with veterans and fellow academy grads and share my experiences and knowledge of business. In some of my business career stops, I was among one of the few veterans in the company.

In 2012, I was invited to join the Wardroom. The Wardroom is a group of Naval Academy graduates in Northern Virginia who are entrepreneurs or business executives who have achieved both leadership success and are accomplished in business.

Fortunately for me, the entrance into this group helped me achieve a reinvigorated level of camaraderie with my fellow graduates and veterans. We all learn from and support each other by acting as a virtual board of directors for the group. Being a part of the Wardroom has been a blessing for me.

I knew after four years of Annapolis there was no doubt that the military was my family and that the camaraderie went deeper than just a friendship because you were living and breathing the military for four years. Obviously, you are getting a world-class education, but you are wearing a uniform and you're experiencing a disciplined, rigorous, military regimen that is both much more demanding and all-encompassing than the curriculum at other universities or institutions.

When I was there, it was very clear and very apparent from day one, and much more apparent as time went on, that you are blazing your own trail that is beyond just your family connection. I knew that this was mine, this was my own connection, I'm a veteran, I always will be, and I'll always be connected to this community.

In March of 2020, I retired from full-time CFO work. Health reasons accelerated my desire to step away from the full-time pressure of being a CFO. I was diagnosed with bladder cancer in March 2018. Fortunately, after two surgeries and ongoing immunotherapy, I have been cancer-free for over two years. My treatment plan and periodic check-ups will continue for seven more years as I am on a ten-year treatment protocol due to the aggressive and recurrent nature of my cancer. Moreover, I have had the great fortune to be married to a marvelous, generous, lady for 26 years, who has supported me through everything. We are both immensely proud of our two sons.

After taking a few months off, my intent was always to start my own business and consult, teach, and volunteer on my own terms. In August, I started my own virtual CFO consulting business. Coincidentally, I knew Mark Mhley as we were both members of the Wardroom. Mark started Re4ormed and was seeking a virtual, fractional CFO offering to add to his slate of services. By the way, Mark coined the name CFO 4Vets. . The idea of supporting veteran-owned and military spouse entrepreneurs greatly appealed to me. I was very enthused to become a part of Mark s creation. This became another terrific way for me to connect further to the veteran community. Thus far, I have only worked with veteran-owned and military spouse businesses. My goal is to dedicate 100% or more of my consultancy work to veteran and military spouse businesses.

Scott Chesson
Lieutenant, USN
U.S. Naval Academy Class of 1984
schess84@cfo4vets.com
Chessolutions LLC | CFO 4Vets
SCOTT CHESSON | LinkedIn

CHAPTER ELEVEN

Stephen White

The Veteran Connection

I coined this expression after witnessing how comfortable over 100 veteran business owners—who were total strangers—were with creating a camaraderie. It was demonstrated at the very first Veteran Business Network (VBN) event held in Manhattan back in the 80 s. Instead of hearing buy my stuff" you heard how can I help you". It was very powerful to me and is the reason that I have pretty much devoted the rest of my business career to assisting veteran entrepreneurship—at a considerable financial cost to me.

I received my Bachelor of Science degree from Florida Southern College in 1966 and was immediately drafted into the Army. I was commissioned after completing Infantry OCS at Fort Benning, GA., and served in Vietnam with the 1st Cavalry Division as a Platoon Leader and Acting Company Commander in 1968 and 1969. The leadership skills I learned while commanding troops in combat have assisted me in a variety of ways every day and immeasurably in my business career.

When we got off of the plane in San Francisco on our return to the states, we were subjected to the jeers of protesters who spit on us as we walked by the fence. Fortunately for them, there was a fence. It was a time of great divide, similar to what we see happening today.

I did not hang with other vets when we came home like you might think. Most of us hid our service, concealed it on job applications and most of us just sucked it up and did not discuss it at all. I m sure that that was a real contributing factor to the level of PTSD suffered by most.

This was when supporting veterans was not cool like it is today. The American Legion did not welcome us, as they did not count Vietnam as a war but as a conflict. Now the Legion is run by Vietnam vets. They always call the WWII guys the greatest generation and maybe they were, but they sure did not step up to help us when we got back. If you ask the post 9/11 troops, they will tell you that it was the Vietnam Vets that were there for them.

Upon my return to civilian life I was a banker in Connecticut and then worked for the Small Business Administration in New Hampshire. I then started a small publishing company with a partner producing small business management material. It was my job to convince banks that by providing information that assisted the growth of small businesses, they could capture more of the small business market. We had over 100 bank clients, but it wasn t working out with my partner, so I left to start my own marketing company.

At the same time, I was asked to start an entrepreneurial training program for Veterans in Manhattan to complement the existing jobs training program at the Veterans Leadership Program. It was really when I got involved with the Veterans Leadership Program that got me back into what I call, vet mode". I was surrounded by veterans, and I was personally making a difference in their lives, it is one of my favorite decisions. In New York City, many veterans had the opportunity to see what we were doing with the Leadership Program and coupled with the VBN, they started coming out of the woodwork! The concept of the Veterans Business Network was born when I saw how many Veteran Owned Businesses were looking for help and a way to connect

This was also around the time I met Mark Hodder of MLH Services who loved the concept of the VBN and jumped in with both feet. We have been partners ever since.

I wrote a series of publications for small business, that was used by a number of banks and I combined them into one that I call Small Business Basics . It was also used by many banks and we produced a special version for SCORE that was sponsored by the Bank of America for a number of years. There were

300,000 copies in English and 150,000 in Spanish distributed throughout the SCORE and B of A offices, nationwide!

Based upon that publication we produced a version for Veterans, uniquely called Basics for Veterans, also a custom version of it for the American Legion and also a guide for Women Veteran Entrepreneurs where we had the input from 5 women who are veteran entrepreneurs. Mark s marketing company, MLH Services, produced these publications in a digital format that was very appealing. (These and other publications are available in both print and digitally as is or customized through the VBN)

I realized during this time, that I had really been missing that camaraderie that is built upon trusting each other with our lives. Sadly, it took corporate America a lot longer to get involved. Personally, I don t care if it s guilt money they are spending or if it s marketing dollars or even if it is sincere—as long as they support the veteran community, it can t be all bad.

I moved from a small town on eastern Long Island (Suffolk County) to SW Florida a little over a year ago. Although I am thoroughly enjoying it down here, I really miss some of my Veteran buddies and one group in particular.

Even though I lived out on the Island, I spent a great deal of time working in NYC and I was proud to be part of what started as the Vietnam Vets Wall Street Holiday lunch—which evolved from a once a year get-together for Vietnam Vets into a quarterly luncheon for combat vets of all eras. It was a blast breaking bread (and washing it down) with great guys!

We also all try to get together for the annual NYC Veterans Day Parade, which I think is the largest Veterans Day Parade in the country. It is always a blast and New York knows how to throw a party or at least they did.

2020 is different, of course. This year I will continue to miss my buddies and reminisce about Veterans Day Parades gone by and will catch up and have a few beers on Veterans Day with some new Legion/VFW buddies down here. (By the way... I don t miss the snow!)

So I ve been involved in one way or another with veteran entrepreneurship for a long time and Mark and I have decided to document this so we will be speaking with some of the real founders of this movement like Rick Weidman and Bill Elmore since we think it s important for today s veteran entrepreneurs to know about how this pathway was created. We all testified before Congress in support of the PL 106-50 or the Veteran Entrepreneurial Act and Small Business Development Act in 1999, helped get it passed and also funded. This law paved the way for all of the Veteran initiatives that have followed.

One of the things I really miss is the VBN networking events we used to hold where 150 to 200 veteran business owners would attend. Just maybe when this Covid deal is over we can get back to that.

The Vet Connection, a cool term that should spark curiosity in veterans and can be used as a way to show what a unique group of veteran entrepreneurs are and how we all want to help, hire and grow other veteran s businesses.

Stephen White
1st Lieutenant USA
First Cavalry Division, Vietnam 1968-1969, Platoon leader/Company Commander, Bronze Star with Combat "V", Purple Heart
Veterans Business Network
Steve@veteransbusinssnetwork.com
https://www.linkedin.com/in/steve-white-13607112/
www.thevbn.us

CHAPTER TWELVE

Suzanne Lesko

I really don't know why it is that all of us are so committed to the sea, except I think it's because in addition to the fact that the sea changes, and the light changes, and ships change, it's because we all came from the sea. And it is an interesting biological fact that all of us have in our veins the exact same percentage of salt in our blood that exists in the ocean, and, therefore, we have salt in our blood, in our sweat, in our tears. We are tied to the ocean. And when we go back to the sea - whether it is to sail or to watch it - we are going back from whence we came."

~John F. Kennedy, Remarks at the Dinner for the America's Cup Crews, September 14, 1962

The sea... the military...our family. No, this is not the tag-line for the next *Fast & Furious* movie – albeit, these are the key factors that I believe have made me the tri-sector leader I am today, and pathway for the evolution of a *Global Solutionista*. In the following pages, you will find my stories and journey of how a girl from Western Pennsylvania made it to the war-room and now the boardroom to help high impact leaders like myself become unstoppable in business and life.

FROM A LOVING CHILDHOOD IN THE STEEL CITY

I am the Founder and Chief Visionary Officer of *Global Solutionista*—an East Coast native who grew up in steel city Pittsburgh, Pennsylvania. I was born into a third-generation family of Slovak descent. Both my grandparents came to the US in the early 1920s to live a better life than in their homeland in the former Czechoslovakia. It was their dream of coming to America that planted the seeds of desire for a better future for our family.

My father was a second-generation immigrant and one of the first in his family to attend college. He received a football scholarship from North Carolina State University and pursued a degree in mechanical engineering. In addition to his athletic pursuits, he had also served in the United States Air Force and was an inspiration for me to follow in his footsteps.

While serving in the Air Force, he met my mother, they fell in love and married soon after. Both my parents paved the way for service and leadership through their roles as servant leaders in the greater Pittsburgh community. We spent many weekends volunteering at soup kitchens, women s shelters and sporting events. I was fortunate to have them as role models throughout my childhood and early adult life, both had a blue-collar work ethic and a white-collar mindset. This mindset helped them navigate the trials and tribulations of the American dream. It was through their years of love and positive mindset that laid the foundation of grit and grace in my life which boded well for my life as an unstoppable leader.

MY PATHWAY INTO THE MILITARY: ANNAPOLIS

Coming from a family of athletes, sports and discipline was a rite of passage for me and entering Annapolis was no different. Swimming was the discipline that helped shape me throughout my formative years and adulthood. I loved being in the water, whether it be the swimming pool, an ocean, or a lake—it s where I felt most free and at one with Mother Nature. I learned to swim by the age of three, and I can remember my parents taking us on a family vacation to Miami Beach.

One afternoon, I climbed the high dive and made it to the edge overlooking the sparkling clear swimming pool below and jumped. I recall feeling invigorated and safely swam to the side to do it again. This kind of gives you the idea of how I knew I was a born-risk taker and what led me to the life I ve lived for most of my adult career. I realized water was the essential element in my pursuit of a life of passion and purpose.

Throughout high school, in addition to swimming, I played golf, and ran track and field. Weekends in Pittsburgh were always busy carpooling with neighborhood kids to their swim meets and other activities. Pittsburgh is also a sports mecca with football, baseball, and hockey along with a culture rich in the arts and many ethnic backgrounds. It s often referred to as the melting pot" city. In addition to sports, I was also exposed to travel, other cultures and international cuisine through my late uncle Richie. He studied art in Florence, Italy and spoke fluent Italian and inspired me to minor in Spanish in college and also study Italian in Florence, Italy years later in my adulthood. It was in these moments of my formative years, that I developed a further passion for travel, culture and food.

Although I enjoy life to the fullest, I also do the hard work, because I knew one day, I wanted to attend university and follow in my father s footsteps. In the early days of high school, I was introduced to our regional *Blue and Gold* officer. A Blue and Gold officer is the liaison between the high school and the Naval Academy and typically guide interested candidates through the admissions process for the Naval Academy.

As a scout for the Naval Academy, our regional *Blue & Gold Officer (BGO),* observed certain candidates in the Greater Pittsburgh area and would reach out when he felt they might be a good fit for the Academy.

One day after swim practice, during my freshman year, the *BGO* approached me and asked if I had considered the Naval Academy. Smelling like chlorine and hair freezing on that crisp winter day, I agreed to learn more about the possibility of attending a service academy.

Prior to this, the thought hadn t crossed my mind. The creative side of me was also interested in art and was considering a Bachelor s in Fine Arts at Carnegie Mellon University, following in the footsteps of my uncle and other family members. My art portfolio had been accepted and I also had a full ride Naval Reserve Officer Training Corps (NROTC) scholarship, but, it wasn t until I visited the Naval Academy in summer 1990 that I felt Annapolis very much aligned with my values and my principles. It was there that I knew that I would be carrying the family tradition of this coveted career. As iron sharpens iron, I knew I would be surrounded by the best and brightest in our nation and be able to contribute to a mission greater than myself.

From 1991 to 1995, I attended the United States Naval Academy in Annapolis, Maryland. I studied Political Science with a minor in Spanish. Those four years were a transformational experience molding and shaping the trajectory for the rest of my life.

POST GRADUATION DUTY AT THE NAVAL ACADEMY

After graduation in May 1995 and before flight school, I was placed on Temporary Assigned Duty (TAD) at the *Yard* (the campus was also referred to as the *Yard*). I was fortunate to work in the *Yard s* Superintendent s office. I can remember our Superintendent at the time sharing with the Brigade, *If you re not having fun, then it s time to move on to something else."* I honestly thought I would do my four years at Annapolis and eight years as a Naval Aviator, and then assess at that point whether to transition to another career or stay in the military on active duty. As a third option, to explore the Reserves, after all, I was still having fun and I knew the military was going to be a lifelong family which would always be a part of my life.

TRAVERSING THE WORLD AS A NAVAL AVIATOR

Shortly after my period at the Superintendent s office in the Fall of 1995, I started my aviation journey in Pensacola, Florida, with Primary Flight Training. I then moved onto Advanced Training at Randolph Air Force Base in San Antonio, Texas where I was winged as a Naval Flight Officer (NFO) in May 1997.

I was one of two women in my graduation class out of about thirty aviators. When you say naval aviation, most people think of *TOPGUN* but, in my case, it was the P-3 Orion community. After going through the Fleet Replacement Squadron (FRS), I was then assigned to an East Coast squadron. Although it was a very challenging few years, I enjoyed the people and the mission.

During one of our early squadron gatherings, referred to as a *hail and farewell"* which is a celebration that builds esprit de corps, I was introduced as *Xena"* along with other new check-ins and their respective call-signs. Needless to say, it was a fun night filled with sea stories and lots of adult beverages. In the years following, I deployed to Europe, Central and South America flying mostly anti-submarine warfare, maritime reconnaissance, surface surveillance, Search and Rescue (SAR), battlegroup support and counter-narcotic missions.

Following my *sea duty* tour on the East Coast, I went onto become a SERE Instructor in Coronado, California on the West Coast. SERE, which stands for Survival Evasion Resistance Escape (SERE) trains selected personnel for the worst conditions they may face in combat. It is a high-risk environment which prepares U.S. military personnel, U.S. Department of Defense civilians, and private military contractors to survive and "return with honor" in survival or captivity scenarios.

It was during this time that I served with Captain Alyce Fernebok, United States Marine Corps (USMC), who is a part of this veteran anthology as well. We had many fun SERE adventures together and also shared similar backgrounds both being Annapolis graduates and female aviators making inroads in an extremely male dominated field.

Those were difficult times, always feeling like we were under the spotlight, but what doesn t kill you makes you stronger in the end.

NAVY RESERVES

After serving over eight years in the aviation community and concluding my SERE duties in Coronado, California, I left active duty in September 2003 and immediately transitioned to the U.S. Navy Reserve on October 1, 2003.

During the fall of 2003, brushfires broke out east of San Diego and slowly moving westward. There was a copper sky over Coronado and, in a way, it was a metaphor for so many things in my life. The power of heat, the transformation melting away one life and entering into a whole new world of service, this time in the U.S. Navy Reserve and a new civilian life.

What I learned from this experience is no matter how much you prepare, you never are really ready and transition is hard in any industry, especially when there s no spare chute.

I had pulled my D-ring by submitting my resignation letter but wasn t quite ready for the actual landing into civilian life and establishing a new routine.

It was a new pathway to a new life, something that I hadn t experienced since I had entered Annapolis on that balmy summer day in July 1991. During this time, that I realized again when defining moments have come to hit you hard and require you to muster your soul s essence, this was definitely one of them.

During my first few years, I was fortunate to work various public affairs engagements and learn the craft. I was always a seeker of the ground truth, and in 2006, I lateral transferred into to the Public Affairs community. My very first combat tour was Baghdad, Iraq in 2007. Hot, gritty, chaotic, Baghdad.

Throughout my Reserve career, including my Iraqi deployment from 2007-2008, there were several times when I was called back to active duty in arduous environments, and I valued those experiences to serve again.

One anchor that helped me was connecting with other transitioning veterans, some who had fully left active duty while others joined the Reserves like myself. This camaraderie innately forms during active duty and is hard to replicate in the civilian world. And it was the connection and camaraderie which later attracted me to work with veterans and other like-minded individuals, such as members of our veteran anthology entrepreneur tribe which I will discuss a bit later in my journey.

It was during one of those times that I reconnected with Lieutenant Commander Lionel Hines and Commander Mark Mhley, both part of this veteran anthology. All three of us served together with Special Operations in 2012 and we were fortunate to work with the finest men and women in our Nation. It was through the examples of both these great Americans that I am here sharing my journey from Plebe Year at Annapolis to the present. Fast forward to 30 years later and that unabashed 18-year-old who entered the *Yard* in 1991 transformed into a Navy Captain leading, mentoring and empowering the next generation of leaders in our great U.S. Navy.

During my leadership journey, I was fortunate to have great mentors throughout the transition that were thought leaders from both the private, public and non-profit sectors. I was able to create balance between going back on active duty and transition back to civilian life with ease. This ability to move back and forth has created connections on all levels across the globe, from U.S. Embassies to Combatant Commands, and it has preserved a bit of the camaraderie that I missed after moving to the Navy Reserve. It truly has been the greatest gift.

THE RISE OF THE GLOBAL SOLUTIONISTA

Perspective is a great thing. There have been many times when I wish I had it when I was an Ensign, but it only came after a cauldron of experiences from the heat of the desert in the Middle East to the jungles of Central America. This ultimately became the genesis for Global Solutionista, a new mission of service where I could take all my experiences and lessons learned in adversity and bring them to high impact leaders through curated experiences.

As Founder and Chief Visionary of Global Solutionista, I help high impact global leaders – including veterans – become unstoppable in business and life. As an advisor, I do this by employing a first-principles approach that reduces seemingly complex problems through their simplest definition to easy to grasp solutions. This process provides a battery of tools and techniques that enable business managers and leaders to capitalize on failure and succeed by becoming more resilient and effective, whether in a war room or in a boardroom.

In addition to Global Solutionista, I also connect with veterans in many ways as well in my civilian world.

I work with a variety of high-impact organizations led by extraordinary veteran leaders. I m also a Managing Director at *Victory Strategies*, a high impact, veteran-owned, leadership collective consultancy consisting of elite mindset practitioners. We improve organizational culture, alignment, and efficiency through leadership development training, advisory and team engagement.

Another organization through which I work with veterans is *Angels 14*, led by an Army and Navy veteran, which makes sure that no one is left behind in our weekly calls for community, camaraderie and connection.

I also support the *GIGO Fund* and swam the Hudson River this past summer helping veterans in need. The GIGO Fund is GI Go Fund is a 501(c)(3) nonprofit charitable organization that assists veterans, active-duty personnel, their family members, veteran supporters, and all members of the military community with finding employment, connecting to their benefits, and accessing housing opportunities.

The event took place on August 7, 2021 honoring the 20-year anniversary of the attacks on September 11, 2001. The swim also recognized the 10-year anniversary of Extortion 17, which involved the tragic loss of a U.S. CH-47 Chinook helicopter carrying 38 service members and crew, resulting in the worst loss of U.S. military life in a single incident in the Afghanistan campaign.

Our team of U.S. Navy SEALs were joined by fellow veterans and patriots in a swim across the Hudson River to honor our military veterans, their families, and all of those who died during 9/11 and the wars that followed that fateful day. The event started in Liberty State Park in New Jersey and concluded in Lower Manhattan to honor the victims of 9/11 and all those who paid the ultimate sacrifice for our country in the wars that followed. It was one of the most epic days in my military career to be surrounded by fellow veterans and supporters.

Just as I jumped in the pool in Miami Beach on that family vacation mentioned earlier, I also jumped about 15 feet into the waters of the Hudson as we began our first leg of the swim. Having just had knee surgery, I wasn't sure how it would hold up, but I knew I couldn't miss an experience which meant so much for the values I live by and what it represented for our country and its heroes that made the ultimate sacrifice. Three miles swimming in the rough currents of the Hudson, we got this!

As one may gather, no one gets you like your veteran family. It s another reason I m honored to have done the Hudson swim together with my fellow veteran tribe and also to experience from the water what my grandparents must have felt coming to Ellis Island many years ago. My eyes teared up as I swam past the Statue of Liberty and just took it all in, swimming with men and women from all different backgrounds, it didn t matter if they were in a different war or experienced other things in their civilian capacity as patriots, there was an unspoken language amongst us all and an instant connection. While we may not have been in combat together or hadn t met previously while serving—we are family. It s an unspoken bond that is unbreakable.

Every day, it s a priority for me to connect with these extraordinary humans through various mediums. It s so important to reach out, to keep in contact, and continue the journey. We are there for each other in this giant family that is created beyond the ranks. There s just nothing quite like it and together we continue the mission one boot at a time.

We are all in, all the time, Godspeed and God Bless America!

Suzanne Lesko is the Founder and President of Global Solutionista, an elite international advisory firm focused on professional management and optimal lifestyle development through bespoke experiences Her mission is to help high impact global leaders – including veterans – be unstoppable in business and life. *She has 20-plus years of experience leading a myriad of defense and national security initiatives and is part of a singular group of women to rise to the rank of Captain in the U.S. Navy* Captain Lesko is a tri-sector leader. She uses her military training, corporate experience, and non-profit leadership to help individuals and organizations survive and thrive in turbulent, demanding, and complex environments. *She takes a holistic approach to all her*

strategic decision making, which enables those involved to perform at the highest level.

Captain Lesko received her commission from the U.S. Naval Academy in 1995. Suzanne is a former U.S. Naval Aviator and is currently serving as a Public Affairs Officer with the U.S. Navy Reserve. She trained America s elite combat teams to perform optimally in high pressure, complex, and hostile situations. Suzanne has also worked as an expert advisor and consultant in stability operations with Grant Thornton in Iraq. She helps the military and veterans by providing high impact leadership training and mentorship to organizations and leaders, as a subject matter expert with Wharton Leadership Ventures, and as a Managing Director with Victory Strategies. Suzanne holds a BS in Political Science from the United States Naval Academy and a MS in Global Leadership from the University of San Diego.

Suzanne Lesko
Captain, USNR
Suzanne Lesko International
suzanne@suzannelesko.com
https://www.linkedin.com/in/suzannelesko
https://linktr.ee/suzannelesko

CHAPTER THIRTEEN

Reserved for Those Who Struggle in Silence

"On the battlefield, the military pledges to leave no soldier behind. As a nation, let it be our pledge that when they return home, we leave no veteran behind."

- Dan Lipinski

To military and veteran families, you give us strength and you have our gratitude.

We reserve this chapter for our brothers and sisters in arms, who struggle in silence, and suffer from physical and mental wounds.

You need not hide in the shadows. Your chapter is yet to be written.

Protecting our freedom and way of life comes at a cost, and you silently bear this burden every day. We, as fellow veterans, commit ourselves to help you out of the shadows, and provide you the support you need to find your purpose, success and happiness, and record your next chapter.

Made in the USA
Middletown, DE
29 November 2021